Machine Learning Basics for Beginners

Prabhakar Veeraraghavan

Published by Bilingual Publication, 2023.

MACHINE LEARNING BASICS FOR BEGINNERS

First edition. November 16, 2023.

ISBN: 979-8223445432

Written by Prabhakar Veeraraghavan.

Table of Contents

....1

Table of Contents 5

Chapter 1.0 Introduction to Machine Learning........................8

1.1 What is Machine Learning? 9

1.2 Machine Learning Definition 10

1.3 Importance of Machine Learning in Today's World.............12

1.4. Scope and Applications of Machine Learning......................13

1.5 Considering the relationship between AI and Machine Learning..17

Chapter 2.0 Foundations of Machine Learning: 20

2.1 Understanding Algorithms: 21

2.2 Data: The Lifeblood of Machine Learning:.................22

2.3 Types of Machine Learning:................................24

2.4 Requirements for creating a good Machine Learning System...27

2.5 How does Machine Learning Work ? 29

Chapter 3.0 Data Preprocessing and Feature Engineering:..........30

3.1 Data Processing:...31

3.2 Handling Missing Values: 35

3.3 Scaling and Normalization: 37

3.4 Feature Selection and Extraction: 39

Chapter 4.0 Building Your First Model:...........................42

4.1 Defining the Problem 43

4.2 Defining Big Data..44

4.3 Considering the sources of Big data.................46

4.4 Understanding the role of Algorithms 48

4.5 Choosing the Right Algorithm: 50

4.6 Training and Testing Data: 52

4.7 Model Evaluation Metrics: 54

Chapter 5.0 Supervised Learning Techniques: 57

5.1 Linear Regression: 58

5.2 Decision Trees and Random Forests: 61

5.3 Support Vector Machines: 64

5.4 Neural Networks: 67

Chapter 6.0 Unsupervised Learning Techniques: 71

6.1 K-Means Clustering and Hierarchical....................................72

6.2. Dimensionality Reduction: Principal Component Analysis (PCA)....................................74

6.3. Anomaly Detection....................................75

Chapter 7.0 Introduction to Deep Learning: 76

7.1 Importance of Deep Learning: 77

7.2 Neural Networks Basics: 79

7.3 Convolutional Neural Networks (CNN): 82

7.4 Recurrent Neural Networks (RNN): 85

7.5 Transfer Learning: 88

Chapter 8.0 Model Deployment and Production:....................90

8.1 Exporting and Saving Models: 91

8.2 Web APIs for Machine Learning: 92

8.3 Considerations for Scalability: 95

Chapter 9.0 Ethical and Responsible Machine Learning:............98

Chapter 11.0 Conclusion: 107

APPENDIX A Glossary of Terms....................................... 110

Appendix B Recommended Books....................................... 112

Machine Learning for Beginners....................................... 113

Advanced Machine Learning Books 114

Appendix C Top 15 Jobs that will be in demand in 2024.......... 115

Machine Learning
Basics
For Beginners

A Comprehensive Guide to
Understanding and Applying
Machine Learning

By :

Prabhakar Veeraraghavan

Machine Learning Basics for Beginners

A Comprehensive Guide to Understanding and Applying Machine Learning

By : Prabhakar Veeraraghavan

**Copyright © 2023
by Prabhakar Veeraraghavan
All rights reserved.
Publication : Bilingual Publication
Type of book**

Unlock the world of Machine Learning with our comprehensive guide for beginners! Dive into the essentials, from algorithms to applications. Perfect for anyone eager to grasp the foundations of ML. Start your journey today. Machine Learning for Beginners, AI Fundamentals Guide, Data Science Basics, Introduction to Deep Learning, Supervised Learning Techniques, Unsupervised Learning Explained, Model Deployment Strategies, Ethical Machine Learning Practices, Future Trends in AI, Beginner-Friendly ML Book, Step-by-Step ML Foundations, Practical Data Preprocessing Tips, Beginner-Friendly ML Book, Responsible AI Learning, Future-Proof Machine Learning

About the author

Prabhakar Veeraraghavan is a Blogger and an accomplished KDP Author after spending more than 2 decades in the corporate world. I am passionate in writing books with an innate ability to transport readers to captivating words and evoke profound emotions.

Combining remarkable creativity with meticulous attention to detail, my idea is to intricate plots that leave readers spellbound from the first page to the last. The motive is not to leave the reads just for the sake of reading but to involve them deep into the subject that have mind blowing effect upon completion of every book.

ALL RIGHTS RESERVED

A Word to the Readers and Writers

Welcome to "**Machine Learning Basics for Beginners**." a Comprehensive Gude to understanding and applying Machine Learning. It is with great excitement and anticipation that I present this e-book, a comprehensive guide designed to unravel the captivating world of **Machine Learning** in the realm of AI and natural language processing.

In the age of Modern computing, Artificial intelligence stands as a remarkable testament to the incredible advancements that we've achieved in the field of technology and **Machine Learning** is a branch of artificial intelligence (AI) and computer science that focuses on the use of data and algorithms to imitate the way that humans learn, by gradually improving its accuracy.

Unlocking The Power of Machine Learning: So, Welcome to a journey that promises to discover the extraordinary world of Machine Learning! This comprehensive guide is crafted especially for beginners, as we embark on a captivating exploration into the realm of intelligent algorithms and data-driven insights.

A Journey of Learning and Discovery: Prepare and make yourself ready to be enthralled as we navigate through the foundations of **Machine Learning**. It's not just about understanding; it's about the exhilarating the process of discovery. Each chapter is a stepping stone, revealing the magic behind algorithms that learn, adapt, and empower us to make sense of the vast sea of data that surrounds us.

What to Expect: In the Chapters that follow, we'll begin with the basics: Understanding Machine Learning from demystifying core concepts to building your first model, expect to witness the transformative power of data in real-time. Dive into the principles of supervised and unsupervised learning, explore the fascinating realm of deep learning, and get a sneak peek into the ethical considerations that shape responsible Machine Learning practices. With Real-world examples that will provide a practical perspective, showing you how Machine Learning can be applied to various fields.

I am sure no where you could find such an easy way of learning with tons of examples that a lay man can even understand from this book. To make things more easier for you, I have also included "**Appendix A** – Glossary of Terms" and "**Appendix B** Recommended Books" and "**Appendix C**" Top 15 Jobs that will be in demand in 2024 is for your ready reference.

The Road Ahead: As you turn the pages, envisage not just a manual but a roadmap—a roadmap that leads you from being a beginner to a confident navigator of the Machine Learning landscape. This journey is yours to Savor, and the road ahead is paved with

Now, dear readers, I invite you to join me on this incredible voyage through the "Basics of Machine Learning for Beginners" Let's embark on a journey of learning, creativity, and innovation that promises to reshape the way we interact with AI and unlock the untold potential of this remarkable technology.

Warmest regards and happy reading!!!

Chapter 1.0 Introduction to Machine Learning

Welcome to the exciting world of **Machine Learning!**

When we say Machine Learning let us understand what do we mean by that? But before we get to know about Machine Learning, let us recap Artificial Intelligence (AI) first.

Artificial Intelligence (AI), a branch of computer science, refers to the stimulation of human intelligence in machines. The cognitive functions of the human brain are studied and replicated on a machine or a system that can mimic human behaviour. Artificial Intelligence is rule-based and static, and it uses logic, if-else rules. It is applied to solve complex problems and automate routine work.

This Artificial Intelligence has a segment called "**Machine Learning**". One of the machine learning subtopics is Deep Learning that follows neural networking. However, in this book, "**Machine Learning Basics Beginners**," we will discuss about the intricacies of this cutting-edge field. Whether you're a curious novice or even a seasoned professional, this guide is crafted to be your companion in unravelling the fundamentals, applications, and ethical considerations that define the landscape of Machine Learning.

But before that let us understand who named the term Machine Learning. The term "Machine Learning" was named by Author Samuel. He is a computer scientist at IBM and Pioneer in AI and computer gaming. Author Samuel designed a computer program for playing checkers. As the program progressed and played many times, it learned from experience using algorithms to make predictions.

1.1 What is Machine Learning?

"Machine learning is like giving computers the ability to learn from experience without being explicitly programmed. Instead of following predefined rules, machines use data to improve their performance over time. It's the technology behind personalized recommendations, voice assistants, and even self-driving cars. In essence, machine learning enables computers to make decisions and predictions by learning from patterns in the data they analyse. It's a powerful tool shaping the future of technology and how we interact with the digital world."

At its core, machine learning is a revolutionary approach to computing that enables systems to learn and improve from experience without explicit programming. Imagine if your computer could evolve, adapt, and make decisions based on patterns and insights it gleans from data—this is the essence of machine learning. It's not just about performing tasks; it's about systems getting smarter over time, making predictions, and continuously refining their understanding of the world.

1.2 Machine Learning Definition

In its raw and basic terms, a "Machine Learning is defined as a set of methodologies that enables the system to automatically learn and improve themselves from various analyses and outputs without being explicitly programmed by a Human interference"

To understand what is exactly is Machine Learning, we can look at it as the science of making computers to learn and act like a brain does or as humans do, and autonomously improve their learning over time by feeding them data. A machine learning process involves using several algorithms to parse data, learn from it, and then make an inference or prediction about something in the world without any explicit rule-based programming.

The basic building blocks of Machine Learning algorithms involve three important components: Viz. –**Representation, Evaluation,** and **Optimization.**

Representation:

In the representation stage, the focus is on how to represent the problem at hand and the data that the machine learning algorithm will learn from. This involves choosing the right features or variables that capture the essential aspects of the problem. Proper representation is crucial because the success of a machine learning model heavily depends on the quality and relevance of the features used to describe the data.

Evaluation:

After the algorithm is trained on the data, it needs to be evaluated to assess its performance. Evaluation involves using a separate set of data (not used during training) to measure how well the model generalizes to new, unseen data. Common evaluation metrics include accuracy, precision, recall, and F1 score, depending on the nature of the problem (classification, regression, etc.). The evaluation stage helps determine whether the algorithm is effective and how well it is expected to perform in real-world scenarios.

Optimization:

Optimization is the process of fine-tuning the algorithm to improve its performance based on the evaluation results. This stage involves adjusting parameters, tweaking the model architecture, or exploring different algorithms to enhance the algorithm's ability to make accurate predictions. The goal is to find the optimal configuration that maximizes the algorithm's effectiveness across various tasks.

In summary, the representation phase sets the stage by defining how the problem and data are presented to the algorithm. The evaluation phase measures how well the algorithm performs on new data, and the optimization phase fine-tunes the algorithm to enhance its performance based on the evaluation results. These three components work in tandem to create a robust and effective machine learning algorithm.

1.3 Importance of Machine Learning in Today's World

Machine Learning (ML) stands as a cornerstone in our digital age, wielding transformative power across various industries and aspects of our daily lives. Its significance lies in its ability to process vast amounts of data, learn patterns, and make predictions or decisions without explicit programming. Here are key reasons why Machine Learning is of paramount importance:

Data Analysis and Pattern Recognition:

Machine Learning excels at sifting through massive datasets to identify patterns that may be impossible for humans to discern. This capability empowers organizations to extract valuable insights, make informed decisions, and gain a competitive edge.

Automation and Efficiency:

ML automates repetitive tasks, enabling businesses to streamline processes and improve efficiency. From data entry to customer support, the automation of routine functions allows human resources to focus on more complex and creative endeavours, fostering innovation.

Personalization and User Experience:

ML is the driving force behind personalized experiences in the digital realm. From product recommendations on e-commerce platforms to tailored content suggestions on streaming services, ML algorithms analyse user behaviour to provide a customized and engaging experience.

Predictive Analytics:

ML's predictive capabilities are instrumental in various fields, including finance, healthcare, and marketing. By analysing historical data, ML models forecast trends, aiding in decision-making processes such as stock investments, patient diagnosis, and targeted marketing strategies.

1.4. Scope and Applications of Machine Learning

The scope of machine learning is vast and ever-expanding. Machine Learning (ML), with its capacity to enable computers to learn from data and improve performance over time, has a vast and expanding scope, permeating through numerous industries. The applications of ML are diverse and continually evolving, promising transformative impacts on the way we work, live, and innovate.

In this section, we navigate through the diverse applications that make machine learning a dynamic and integral part of our digital ecosystem. From image and speech recognition to predicting stock market trends and diagnosing medical conditions, machine learning algorithms are at the heart of groundbreaking solutions.

Data Analysis and Predictive Modelling:

ML excels in data analysis, allowing organizations to extract meaningful insights and predict future trends. From financial forecasting to demand planning, ML models analyse historical data to make accurate predictions, aiding in informed decision-making.

Healthcare and Medicine:

In healthcare, ML is revolutionizing patient care, diagnosis, and treatment. ML algorithms analyze patient data to identify patterns, predict disease outcomes, and recommend personalized treatment plans. This application holds the potential to enhance medical decision-making and improve patient outcomes.

Finance and Banking:

ML is widely used in the finance sector for fraud detection, risk assessment, and algorithmic trading. Its ability to analyse vast datasets in real-time enables financial institutions to make quicker and more accurate decisions, minimizing risks and optimizing investment strategies.

E-commerce and Recommendation Systems:

E-commerce platforms leverage ML to provide personalized recommendations based on user behaviour. These recommendation systems enhance the user experience, increase customer satisfaction, and drive sales by presenting products or content tailored to individual preferences.

Natural Language Processing (NLP):

ML powers NLP, enabling computers to understand, interpret, and generate human-like text. Applications range from virtual assistants like Siri and Alexa to sentiment analysis in social media, making human-computer interaction more natural and effective.

Autonomous Vehicles and Robotics:

ML plays a crucial role in the development of autonomous systems, including self-driving cars and drones. These systems use ML algorithms to interpret sensory data, navigate environments, and make real-time decisions, contributing to the advancement of transportation and robotics.

Manufacturing and Industry 4.0:

In manufacturing, ML enhances efficiency through predictive maintenance, quality control, and supply chain optimization. By analysing sensor data, ML models can predict equipment failures, reduce downtime, and optimize production processes in the era of Industry 4.0.

Cybersecurity:

ML strengthens cybersecurity by identifying and responding to potential threats in real-time. ML algorithms can analyse patterns in network traffic, detect anomalies, and enhance security measures to protect against cyber attacks and data breaches.

Environmental Monitoring and Climate Modelling:

ML contributes to environmental science by analysing vast datasets related to climate and ecological systems. It aids in climate modelling, predicting natural disasters, and optimizing resource management for sustainable development.

Education and Personalized Learning:

In education, ML facilitates personalized learning experiences by adapting educational content to individual student needs. Learning platforms use ML algorithms to analyse student performance data and provide tailored recommendations for optimal learning outcomes.

As ML technologies continue to advance, the scope and applications of Machine Learning are set to expand further. From optimizing business processes to addressing global challenges, ML is at the forefront of innovation, shaping a future where intelligent systems enhance efficiency, foster discovery, and contribute to the betterment of society as a whole.

Innovation and Exploration:

The continued development of ML technologies fuels innovation across diverse industries. From robotics to natural language processing, ML opens doors to new possibilities, pushing the boundaries of what is achievable in the realms of technology and human-machine interaction.

In essence, Machine Learning is not just a tool but a catalyst for progress, revolutionizing how we interact with information, make decisions, and address challenges. Its importance lies in its capacity to enhance efficiency, provide personalized experiences, and contribute to the advancement of society across various domains. As we embrace the era of intelligent machines, the impact and importance of Machine Learning are set to expand, shaping the future in ways we are only beginning to fathom.

I hope after reading the first Chapter, you would have understood not only the theoretical foundations of Machine Learning but also appreciate its real-world significance and envision the limitless possibilities it holds for the future. So, let's dive in and unravel more about the mysteries of machine learning together!

1.5 Considering the relationship between AI and Machine Learning.

Artificial Intelligence (AI) and Machine Learning (ML) are often used interchangeably, but they represent distinct yet interconnected concepts within the realm of technology. To comprehend their relationship, it's crucial to recognize the broader scope of AI and the specific role that ML plays within it.

AI as the Umbrella Term:

Artificial Intelligence refers to the overarching concept of creating machines or systems that can perform tasks requiring human-like intelligence. These tasks encompass a broad spectrum, from basic rule-based decision-making to complex problem-solving and learning from experience.

Machine Learning as a Subset of AI:

Machine Learning is a subset of AI, focusing on the development of algorithms and models that enable computers to learn and improve without explicit programming. In essence, ML is an approach to achieving AI by providing systems with the ability to learn patterns and make predictions based on data.

The Learning Aspect:

The fundamental distinction lies in the learning aspect. While AI encompasses a range of techniques for mimicking human intelligence, ML specifically deals with algorithms that learn and adapt. Instead of relying on explicit programming for every scenario, ML systems learn from data and experiences.

Types of AI and ML:

AI can be categorized into Narrow or Weak AI, which is designed for a specific task, and General or Strong AI, which aims to replicate human-like intelligence across various tasks. ML, on the other hand, can be categorized into supervised learning, unsupervised learning, and reinforcement learning, each serving different purposes in the learning process.

Training and Adaptation:

In ML, the model undergoes a training phase where it learns patterns and relationships within the provided data. This trained model can then be applied to new, unseen data, adapting and improving its performance over time. AI, in a broader sense, may involve rule-based systems that do not necessarily learn but follow predetermined instructions.

AI without ML:

Not all AI systems incorporate Machine Learning. Some AI applications are rule-based, where explicit programming dictates the system's behaviour. These systems lack the adaptability and learning capabilities associated with ML but can still perform specific tasks effectively.

Synergy in Practice:

While ML is a subset of AI, the two concepts often work in tandem. ML provides the learning capabilities that contribute to the development of intelligent systems under the broader umbrella of AI. Many contemporary AI applications leverage ML algorithms to enhance their functionality, adapt to changing conditions, and improve performance over time.

The Evolutionary Link:

As technology advances, the relationship between AI and ML evolves. Early AI systems were predominantly rule-based, but the integration of ML has led to more flexible and adaptive AI solutions. The synergy between AI and ML continues to drive innovation and push the boundaries of what intelligent systems can achieve.

In summary, while Artificial Intelligence encompasses a wide range of techniques to simulate human-like intelligence, Machine Learning is a specialized approach within AI that focuses on enabling computers to learn and adapt from data. The relationship between AI and ML is symbiotic, with ML serving as a key tool to achieve intelligent behaviour within AI systems. Together, they pave the way for the development of sophisticated technologies that have the potential to reshape how we interact with and benefit from intelligent machines.

Chapter 2.0 Foundations of Machine Learning:

The foundations of Machine Learning (ML) are like the building blocks that help computers learn and make decisions without explicit programming. At the core, there are algorithms, which are step-by-step instructions that guide machines through the learning process. Data is the lifeblood of ML, providing the examples and patterns for machines to recognize and understand.

Features within the data are like the ingredients in a recipe, highlighting the important aspects for the machine to focus on. Training is the practice session where machines refine their abilities by learning from data. Think of it like teaching a dog new trick – the more examples (data) and practice (training), the better the machine gets at predicting, classifying, or making decisions.

Evaluation is like testing the dog's performance, ensuring the machine has truly mastered its task. These foundational elements come together, creating the magic of machines learning from experience.

In simple terms, Machine learning stands on a sturdy foundation built upon key principles, algorithms, and a profound understanding of data. This chapter serves as the cornerstone of your journey into the world of machine learning, laying the groundwork for comprehending its intricacies.

2.1 Understanding Algorithms:

Algorithms are like recipes for computers. They are sets of step-by-step instructions designed to solve specific problems or perform particular tasks. Just as a cooking recipe guides you through the process of making a dish, an algorithm tells a computer exactly what operations to carry out in order to achieve a desired outcome. Whether it's sorting a list of numbers, searching for information on the internet, or making predictions based on data, algorithms are the behind-the-scenes wizards that make our digital world work. They come in all shapes and sizes, each tailored to tackle different challenges and help computers make sense of the vast amounts of information they encounter.

In this section, we embark on a journey through various algorithms, dissecting their functionalities and understanding how they contribute to the learning process. Whether it's the simplicity of linear regression or the complexity of neural networks, we explore how algorithms process information, identify patterns, and make predictions. By the end of this section, you'll gain a solid grasp of the diverse toolbox of algorithms that machine learning leverages.

2.2 Data: The Lifeblood of Machine Learning:

Data plays a pivotal role and are "The Lifeblood of Machine Learning" emphasizes the critical role that data plays in the functioning and success of machine learning systems. In the context of machine learning, data serves as the foundation upon which algorithms learn, generalize, and make predictions. Here's a detailed explanation of why data is considered the lifeblood:

Training Machine Learning Models: Machine learning models learn from examples. These examples, or data points, consist of input features and corresponding outputs. During the training phase, algorithms analyse this labelled data to discern patterns, relationships, and trends.

Learning Patterns and Representations: The richness and diversity of the data directly impact the model's ability to learn meaningful patterns. High-quality, diverse data allows algorithms to capture a wide range of scenarios, enabling better generalization to new, unseen data.

Supervised Learning with Labelled Data: In supervised learning, where the algorithm is provided with labelled training data (input-output pairs), the model learns to map inputs to outputs. The accuracy and representativeness of this labelled data significantly influence the model's performance and predictive capabilities.

Unsupervised Learning with Unlabelled Data: Unsupervised learning algorithms, which operate on unlabelled data, rely on the inherent structures and relationships within the data. Clustering algorithms, for example, group similar data points, uncovering hidden patterns without explicit guidance.

Testing and Validation: The model's performance is assessed using additional data not seen during training. This testing phase ensures that the model can generalize well to new, unseen instances. The quality of the testing data is crucial in evaluating the model's robustness and reliability.

Real-world Applications: In real-world applications, the quality of the data directly impacts the performance of machine learning models. For instance, in healthcare, accurate and diverse patient data is crucial for developing effective diagnostic models.

Ethical Considerations: The data used in machine learning also raises ethical considerations. Biases in training data can lead to biased models, reinforcing and potentially exacerbating existing societal prejudices. Therefore, understanding and addressing biases in the data is essential for responsible machine learning.

The success of machine learning systems is intrinsically tied to the quality, quantity, and representativeness of the data they are trained on. Like blood nourishing a living organism, data fuels the learning process, enabling machines to comprehend, adapt, and make informed decisions in diverse and dynamic environments.

2.3 Types of Machine Learning:

Now let us go further deep into the subject. Machine learning can be broadly categorized into three main types based on the learning approach via., Supervised learning, Unsupervised learning, and Reinforcement learning.

<u>**Supervised Learning:**</u>

Meaning : In supervised learning, models are trained on labelled datasets, where the algorithm learns to map input data to corresponding output labels. We explore the applications of supervised learning in tasks like image classification, language translation, and predicting outcomes.

Description: In supervised learning, the algorithm is trained on a labelled dataset, where each input is paired with the corresponding desired output. The goal is for the algorithm to learn a mapping function that can predict the output for new, unseen inputs.

Use Cases: Commonly used for classification and regression tasks. Examples include image recognition, spam detection, and predicting house prices, Email Spam Detection, Risk Assessment and Score Prediction.

<u>**Unsupervised Learning:**</u>

Meaning : Unsupervised learning operates without labelled output, focusing on identifying patterns and structures within data. Clustering and dimensionality reduction are key components explored here, showcasing how algorithms can uncover hidden relationships and groupings in datasets.

Description: Unsupervised learning deals with unlabelled data, where the algorithm tries to find patterns, structures, or relationships without explicit guidance. The system aims to explore the inherent structure within the data.

Use Cases: Clustering, dimensionality reduction, and association rule learning. Examples include customer segmentation, anomaly detection, and topic modelling, Text Mining, Face Recognition, Big Data Visualization, Image Recognition.

<u>Reinforcement Learning:</u>

Meaning : Inspired by behavioural psychology, reinforcement learning involves agents learning through trial and error. We delve into the concepts of rewards, penalties, and the iterative learning process that characterizes reinforcement learning. Applications, such as game playing and robotic control, illustrate the versatility and potential of this learning paradigm.

Description: Reinforcement learning involves an agent that learns to make decisions by interacting with an environment. The agent receives feedback in the form of rewards or penalties, allowing it to learn optimal strategies through a trial-and-error process.

Use Cases: Commonly applied in areas where decision-making is crucial, such as robotics, game playing, and autonomous systems like self-driving cars, Finance Sector, Inventory management, and Robot Navigation.

These three types of Machine Learning can further be categorized into other specialized approaches and techniques:

<u>Semi-supervised Learning:</u>

Description: This type combines elements of both supervised and unsupervised learning. The algorithm is trained on a dataset that contains both labelled and unlabelled data, leveraging the advantages of both approaches.

Use Cases: Useful when acquiring labelled data is expensive or time-consuming. Examples include speech recognition and natural language processing.

<u>Self-supervised Learning:</u>

Description: In self-supervised learning, models are trained using the data itself to generate labels, often by creating tasks that don't require external labelling.

Use Cases: Widely used in pre-training models for natural language understanding and computer vision tasks.

<u>Transfer Learning</u>

Description: Transfer learning involves training a model on one task and then using the knowledge gained to improve performance on a related task.

Use Cases: Efficiently applies knowledge gained from one domain to another, such as using a pre-trained image recognition model for a new but related image classification task.

Note that these various types of machine learning cater to different problem domains and scenarios, offering flexibility and adaptability to a wide range of applications.

I hope after reading this Chapter, you will have a comprehensive understanding of the building blocks that constitute the machine learning landscape. Armed with knowledge about algorithms, the pivotal role of data, and the diverse learning paradigms, they are well-prepared to delve into the practical aspects of implementing machine learning solutions. This chapter lays the groundwork for the subsequent exploration of data preprocessing, model building, and ethical considerations in the fascinating world of machine learning.

2.4 Requirements for creating a good Machine Learning System

Creating a good Machine Learning Systems requires careful planning and consideration of various aspects, encompassing data, algorithms, and infrastructure. Here is a list of key requirements that has to be considered :

High-Quality Data: Good machine learning systems start with high-quality, relevant, and representative data. The data should cover a diverse range of scenarios and be free from biases that might affect the model's performance.

Data Preprocessing: Before feeding data into machine learning algorithms, preprocessing steps are essential. This includes handling missing values, scaling features, and encoding categorical variables to ensure the data is in a suitable format for training.

Feature Engineering: Selecting and transforming relevant features from the data can significantly impact model performance. Feature engineering involves creating new features or transforming existing ones to enhance the model's ability to learn patterns.

Appropriate Algorithms: Choosing the right machine learning algorithm for the task at hand is crucial. Different algorithms are suitable for different types of problems, and experimentation may be needed to find the most effective one.

Model Training and Evaluation: Rigorous model training and evaluation are essential. This involves splitting the data into training and testing sets, training the model on the training set, and evaluating its performance on the testing set to ensure it generalizes well to new data.

Hyperparameter Tuning: Adjusting hyperparameters, which are parameters external to the model that control its learning process, is crucial for optimizing performance. Grid search or randomized search can be employed to find the best hyperparameter values.

Cross-Validation: Cross-validation helps assess how well a model will generalize to an independent dataset. Techniques like k-fold cross-validation ensure robust model performance evaluation.

Regularization Techniques: Regularization methods, such as L1 and L2 regularization, help prevent overfitting by penalizing overly complex models. These techniques contribute to models that generalize well to unseen data.

Scalability and Efficiency: Machine learning systems should be scalable to handle large datasets and efficient in terms of computation. This is particularly important when deploying models in real-world applications.

Interpretability and Explain-ability: Understanding and interpreting model decisions are crucial, especially in sensitive domains. Ensuring that models are interpretable and explainable can enhance trust and facilitate decision-making.

Robustness to Noise and Adversarial Attacks: Good machine learning systems are robust to noise in the data and resilient to adversarial attacks. Robust models are more likely to perform well in real-world, dynamic environments.

Ethical Considerations: Consider the ethical implications of the data and models, addressing issues such as fairness, transparency, and bias. Ensure that the machine learning system aligns with ethical standards and legal regulations.

Continuous Monitoring and Updating: Machine learning models should be continuously monitored in production to ensure they adapt to changes in the data distribution. Regular updates and retraining may be necessary to maintain optimal performance.

By addressing the above-mentioned requirements, developers and data scientists can build a Solid Machine Learning Systems that are accurate, reliable, and applicable to real-world problems.

2.5 How does Machine Learning Work ?

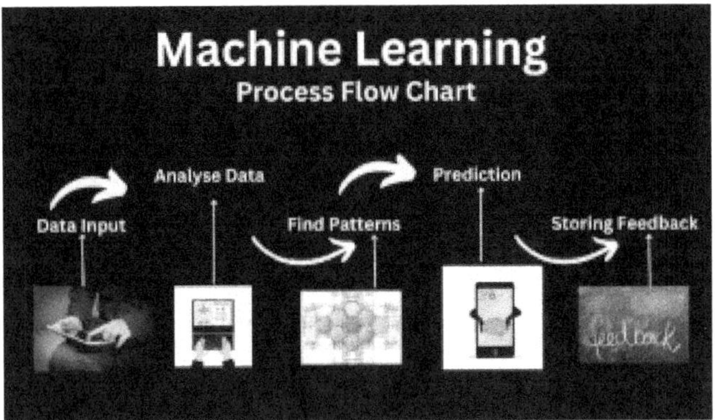

Now how does Machine Learning Work ? Machine Learning uses the processes those are similar to that of data mining. It is for this reason, that Machine Learning algorithms are described in terms of target function(f) that maps input variable (x) to an output variable (y). Mathematically, this can be represented as: $y=f(x)$, where Out variable (y) is the outcome of input variable (x).

There is one more variable called error (e) which is independent of the input variable x. Therefore the generalized form of the equation can be written as $y=f(x) + e$ and this includes the error portion.

In Machine Learning the mapping from x to y is done for getting the predictions. Hence this method is called as predictive modelling that makes most accurate predictions.

Chapter 3.0 Data Preprocessing and Feature Engineering:

With a solid understanding of the foundations laid in the previous chapter, we now venture into the crucial phase of preparing data for machine learning. Data preprocessing is akin to cleaning and refining raw materials before crafting a masterpiece. In this chapter, we explore the essential steps involved in transforming raw data into a format suitable for training robust machine learning models.

3.1 Data Processing:

Data processing refers to the manipulation and transformation of raw data into a more meaningful and useful format. Data processing is a fundamental aspect of information systems and is crucial for deriving actionable insights from the vast amounts of data generated in various domains. It involves a series of operations that convert input data into desired output, often with the goal of extracting valuable information, making it suitable for analysis, or preparing it for further use in various applications. Data processing can take place at different stages, including data collection, storage, retrieval, and analysis. The process typically includes several key steps:

Let's delve into each of the Keh steps of data processing in more detail:

Data Collection:

Definition: Data collection is the process of gathering raw information from various sources, such as sensors, databases, surveys, or external systems.

Details: This phase involves identifying the sources of data, determining what data is relevant to the analysis or application, and extracting the necessary information. It could involve automated processes, manual input, or a combination of both.

Data Cleaning:

Definition: Data cleaning, or data cleansing, is the process of identifying and correcting errors, inconsistencies, or missing values in the collected data.

Details: Errors may include typos, outliers, or inaccuracies. Missing values might be filled through imputation or excluded based on the extent of their impact. Clean data is essential for accurate analysis and reliable results.

Data Transformation:

Definition: Data transformation involves converting raw data into a suitable format for analysis or application.

Details: This step includes normalizing numerical values (putting them on a similar scale), scaling features, and encoding categorical variables. The goal is to prepare the data for the specific requirements of the analysis or model being used.

Data Integration:

Definition: Data integration is the process of combining data from multiple sources to create a unified dataset.

Details: Integration helps provide a comprehensive view by combining diverse datasets. This may involve resolving schema mismatches, standardizing units of measurement, and addressing other issues to ensure a coherent dataset.

Data Aggregation:

Definition: Data aggregation involves grouping and summarizing data to obtain a higher-level view.

Details: Aggregation might include tasks like averaging, summing, or counting data to create summaries or aggregates. This is particularly useful when dealing with large datasets or when the analysis requires a broader perspective.

Data Storage:

Definition: Data storage is the process of saving processed data in a structured manner, typically in databases, data warehouses, or other storage systems.

Details: Storage involves decisions about the type of database, data structure, and indexing methods. It ensures efficient and secure retrieval of data when needed.

Data Retrieval:

Definition: Data retrieval is the process of accessing and extracting specific subsets of data for analysis or reporting.

Details: Retrieval involves querying databases or data repositories to obtain the necessary information. This step is crucial for obtaining the data required for analysis or generating reports.

Data Analysis:

Definition: Data analysis involves applying statistical, mathematical, or machine learning techniques to extract insights, patterns, or trends from the processed data.

Details: This phase includes exploratory data analysis, hypothesis testing, and model building. The goal is to gain a deeper understanding of the data and extract valuable information.

Data Presentation:

Definition: Data presentation is the communication of analysis results in a comprehensible and visually appealing manner.

Details: This could involve creating charts, graphs, dashboards, or reports to convey the insights derived from the analysis. Effective data presentation is crucial for decision-makers to understand and act upon the findings.

Please note that each of these steps is integral to the overall data processing pipeline, and the success of subsequent stages often depends on the quality and accuracy achieved in the preceding steps. Efficient and effective data processing is essential for organizations and researchers to leverage the full potential of their data for informed decision-making and problem-solving.

3.2 Handling Missing Values:

Handling missing values is a crucial step in data preprocessing to ensure that data is complete and suitable for analysis or machine learning tasks. Missing values can occur for various reasons, such as errors in data collection, sensor malfunctions, or intentional omissions. Dealing with missing values requires careful consideration, and there are several strategies to address them:

<u>Deletion of Missing Values:</u>

Complete Case Analysis: This involves removing entire rows of data that contain missing values. While straightforward, it may result in a significant loss of information, especially if many rows have missing values.

<u>Imputation:</u>

Mean, Median, or Mode Imputation: Replace missing values with the mean, median, or mode of the observed values in the variable. This is a simple method but may not be suitable if the data has outliers.

Forward Fill or Backward Fill (Time-Series Data): Use the value before or after the missing value to fill it, particularly applicable in time-series data.

Linear Regression Imputation: Predict missing values using a linear regression model based on other variables in the dataset.

K-Nearest Neighbours (KNN) Imputation: Estimate missing values by considering the values of their k-nearest neighbours in the feature space.

<u>Advanced Imputation Techniques:</u>

Multiple Imputation: Generate multiple imputations for each missing value, considering the uncertainty associated with imputation. This is particularly useful for handling the variability in imputed values.

Matrix Factorization Techniques: Use methods like Singular Value Decomposition (SVD) to decompose the data matrix into factors, enabling the estimation of missing values.

<u>Domain-Specific Imputation:</u>

Custom Imputation Strategies: Depending on the nature of the data and the domain knowledge, create custom strategies for imputing missing values. This could involve more sophisticated methods tailored to the specific characteristics of the dataset.

Indicator Variables:

Flagging Missing Values: Introduce a binary indicator variable to denote whether a value is missing in a particular observation. This allows the model to recognize and potentially account for missingness as a separate feature.

The choice of method depends on the nature of the data, the proportion of missing values, and the specific requirements of the analysis or modelling task. It's essential to carefully evaluate the impact of the chosen strategy on the quality and validity of the data. Additionally, documenting the approach taken in handling missing values is crucial for transparency and reproducibility in data analysis or machine learning projects.

Missing data is a common challenge in real-world datasets. We delve into strategies for handling missing values, whether through imputation techniques, removing affected samples, or leveraging advanced algorithms to fill in the gaps.

3.3 Scaling and Normalization:

Scaling and normalization ensure that features within the dataset are on a similar scale, preventing certain features from dominating the learning process due to their larger magnitude. We explore methods like Min-Max scaling and Z-score normalization to achieve this balance.

Data Scaling:

Data scaling is a preprocessing technique used to standardize the range of independent variables or features of a dataset. The objective is to ensure that all variables have the same scale, preventing certain features from dominating others. This is particularly important for algorithms that are sensitive to the scale of input features, such as gradient-based optimization algorithms in machine learning.

There are different methods for scaling data:

<u>Min-Max Scaling (Normalization):</u> This method scales the data to a specific range, usually between 0 and 1. The formula for min-max scaling is:

X Scaled = <u>X-min (X)</u>

Max (X) – Min (X)

Where X is the original data point, min(X) is the minimum value in the feature, and max(X) is the maximum value in the feature.

<u>Standardization (Z-score normalization):</u> This method scales the data to have a mean (u) of 0 and a standard deviation (σ) of 1. The formula for standardization is:

X standardized = <u>X - μ</u>

σ

Standardization assumes that the data follows a normal distribution.

<u>Robust Scaling</u>: This method uses the median and interquartile range (IQR) to scale the data, making it robust to outliers. The formula is similar to standardization but uses the median and IQR instead of the mean and standard deviation.

X robust =X – <u>median (X)</u>

   IQR(x)

Normalization:

Normalization, often used interchangeably with min-max scaling, specifically refers to scaling data to a range between 0 and 1. The goal is to transform the features so that they share a common scale and are within a similar numerical range.

Normalization is especially useful when the features have different units or when working with algorithms that rely on distances between data points, such as k-nearest neighbours or support vector machines. By bringing all features into the same scale, normalization ensures that each feature contributes proportionally to the model's learning process.

In summary, both data scaling and normalization aim to make the features of a dataset comparable, preventing certain features from disproportionately influencing machine learning algorithms. The choice between methods depends on the characteristics of the data and the requirements of the specific algorithm being used.

3.4 Feature Selection and Extraction:

Not all features are created equal. Some may contribute significantly to the model's performance, while others might introduce noise. We explore techniques for feature selection, choosing the most relevant features. Additionally, we delve into feature extraction methods, transforming existing features into a more informative representation.

Feature Selection:

Feature selection is the process of choosing a subset of relevant and significant features from a larger set of features in a dataset. The goal is to improve the performance of a model by reducing overfitting, improving interpretability, and often speeding up the training process. Here are some common techniques for feature selection:

<u>Filter Methods:</u>

Correlation-Based Methods: Select features that have the highest correlation with the target variable. Features that are highly correlated with the target are considered more informative.

Statistical Tests (e.g., chi-squared test): Evaluate the statistical significance of each feature with respect to the target variable and select the most informative ones.

<u>Wrapper Methods:</u>

Forward Selection: Start with an empty set of features and iteratively add the most beneficial feature at each step based on model performance.

Backward Elimination: Begin with all features and iteratively remove the least valuable feature based on model performance.

Recursive Feature Elimination (RFE): Use a model to recursively remove the least important features until the desired number of features is reached.

<u>Embedded Methods:</u>

Regularization (L1 or L2 regularization): Include a penalty term in the model's objective function, which encourages the model to use fewer features. This is particularly common in linear models like Lasso regression.

Tree-based Methods: Decision trees and ensemble methods (e.g., Random Forest) inherently perform feature selection by selecting the most informative features during the tree-building process.

Dimensionality Reduction:

Principal Component Analysis (PCA): Transform the original features into a new set of uncorrelated features (principal components) that capture most of the variance in the data.

Linear Discriminant Analysis (LDA): Similar to PCA but takes into account class labels, making it suitable for classification problems.

Feature Extraction:

Feature extraction involves transforming the original features into a new set of features that captures essential information while reducing dimensionality. Unlike feature selection, feature extraction creates entirely new features. Common techniques for feature extraction include:

Principal Component Analysis (PCA):

Dimensionality Reduction: PCA is both a feature selection and feature extraction technique. It transforms the data into a new set of uncorrelated features, allowing for dimensionality reduction.

Linear Discriminant Analysis (LDA):

Discriminative Features: LDA aims to find the linear combinations of features that best discriminate between different classes. It is particularly useful for classification tasks.

t-Distributed Stochastic Neighbor Embedding (t-SNE):

Non-linear Dimensionality Reduction: t-SNE is effective at visualizing high-dimensional data in two or three dimensions, preserving local relationships between data points.

Autoencoders:

Neural Network-Based: Autoencoders are neural network architectures that learn to encode input data into a lower-dimensional representation, which can serve as a feature extraction mechanism.

Factor Analysis:

Latent Factors: Factor analysis models observed variables as linear combinations of underlying latent factors. It is useful for identifying hidden structures in the data.

The choice between feature selection and feature extraction depends on the specific characteristics of the dataset, the modelling task, and the interpretability of the transformed features. Feature selection is more concerned with choosing a subset of existing features, while feature extraction involves creating entirely new features based on the original ones.

Chapter 4.0 Building Your First Model:

Armed with a well-prepared dataset, we move on to the exciting phase of building machine learning models. In this chapter, we guide you through the process of selecting the right algorithm, training your model, and evaluating its performance.

4.1 Defining the Problem

Defining the problem is a foundational step in any data science or machine learning endeavour, requiring a meticulous examination of the project's objectives and parameters. This involves clearly articulating the specific goal or challenge the project aims to address, such as predicting customer churn, image classification, or process optimization. The scope of the problem is meticulously outlined to determine which components are included and which are excluded.

Understanding the required data is imperative, as it dictates the features relevant to the task, and decisions regarding data availability or the need for additional collection must be made. Establishing measurable success criteria is fundamental, delineating the metrics by which the project's success will be evaluated, whether through accuracy, precision, recall, or other relevant measures. Identifying key stakeholders and considering their perspectives is crucial, ensuring the project aligns with the needs of end-users, decision-makers, and other individuals affected by or involved in the initiative.

Moreover, the problem definition necessitates an examination of constraints, be they financial, temporal, or legal, as well as an assessment of potential ethical considerations such as privacy, bias, and fairness. A review of existing literature provides valuable insights, helping avoid redundant efforts and informing the project's direction.

Recognizing the iterative nature of problem definition is essential, allowing for adjustments as insights and information evolve. Risk assessment is integrated into the process, identifying potential challenges like data quality issues or interpretability challenges. Finally, effective communication of the problem statement is paramount, serving as a guiding document throughout the project and ensuring alignment among team members and stakeholders.

4.2 Defining Big Data

Big Data refers to extremely large and complex datasets that cannot be easily managed, processed, or analysed using traditional data processing tools or methods. Big Data is characterized by the three Vs:

Volume:

Definition: Refers to the sheer size of the data. Big Data involves datasets that are too large to be comfortably processed by conventional databases and software tools.

Example: Terabytes, petabytes, or even exabytes of data generated by social media interactions, sensor data, financial transactions, and more.

Velocity:

Definition: Indicates the speed at which data is generated, collected, and processed. Big Data often involves data streams that arrive rapidly and require real-time or near-real-time processing.

Example: Continuous streams of social media updates, real-time financial transactions, or sensor data from the Internet of Things (IoT) devices

Variety:

Definition: Encompasses the diverse types of data formats and sources. Big Data includes structured, semi-structured, and unstructured data from a variety of sources.

Example: Structured data from databases, semi-structured data like JSON or XML files, and unstructured data such as text documents, images, audio, and video.

Additionally, some extensions to the three Vs have been proposed to further describe Big Data:

Veracity:

Definition: Refers to the quality and reliability of the data. Big Data often involves dealing with data from various sources, and ensuring data accuracy and reliability can be challenging.

Example: Dealing with data from social media where information may be inaccurate or incomplete.

Variability:

Definition: Describes the inconsistency in the data flow. Big Data sources may produce data with varying levels of consistency and quality.

Example: Fluctuations in the data flow from sensors due to changes in environmental conditions.

Value:

Definition: Emphasizes the importance of extracting valuable insights and knowledge from Big Data to make informed decisions.

Example: Using Big Data analytics to derive business intelligence, optimize processes, or gain a competitive advantage.

To effectively manage and derive insights from Big Data, specialized tools and technologies, such as distributed computing frameworks (e.g., Apache Hadoop, Apache Spark), NoSQL databases, and advanced analytics algorithms, are commonly employed. The challenges and opportunities presented by Big Data have significant implications across various industries, including finance, healthcare, telecommunications, and more, where the ability to analyse vast amounts of data can lead to valuable insights and innovations.

4.3 Considering the sources of Big data

Considering the sources of Big Data involves understanding where and how large volumes of complex data are generated. Big Data comes from various sources, and these sources can be broadly categorized into three main types:

<u>Traditional Sources:</u>

These are sources of data that have been traditionally used and are well-established. Examples include:

Databases: Relational databases, SQL databases, and other structured data sources that have been in use for years.

Enterprise Systems: Data generated from enterprise resource planning (ERP) systems, customer relationship management (CRM) systems, and other business applications.

Logs and Files: Server logs, application logs, and various file formats containing historical records and information.

<u>New Age Digital Sources:</u>

With the rise of digital technologies, a significant portion of Big Data comes from digital platforms and interactions. Examples include:

Social Media: Data generated from social media platforms, including text posts, images, videos, and user interactions.

Mobile Devices: Information from mobile applications, sensors, and location-based services.

Web and Clickstream Data: Data generated from website interactions, clicks, and online activities.

<u>Emerging Sources:</u>

As technology advances, new sources of Big Data continue to emerge. These include:

Internet of Things (IoT): Data from interconnected devices and sensors, such as smart appliances, wearable devices, and industrial sensors.

Machine-generated Data: Information produced by machines and automated systems, such as data from manufacturing equipment, connected vehicles, or smart infrastructure.

Biometric Data: Data generated from biometric sensors, including fingerprints, facial recognition, and other biometric identification methods.

Understanding the diverse origins of Big Data is crucial for effectively managing, processing, and deriving insights from these massive datasets. Each source presents unique challenges and opportunities, and businesses and organizations need to adapt their data strategies to harness the value that Big Data offers from these various channels.

4.4 Understanding the role of Algorithms

Algorithms are sets of instructions or rules that computers follow to perform specific tasks or solve particular problems. They serve as the computational procedures that guide the step-by-step execution of a task

Understanding the role of algorithms is fundamental in the context of data science and machine learning. An algorithm is a step-by-step set of instructions or rules that a computer follows to solve a specific problem or perform a particular task. In the realm of data science and machine learning, algorithms play a central role in extracting patterns, making predictions, and automating decision-making processes. Here are key aspects of the role of algorithms in this context:

Pattern Recognition: Algorithms are designed to recognize patterns within data. They can identify trends, correlations, and structures that might be challenging or impossible for humans to discern in large and complex datasets. This capability is crucial for tasks such as image recognition, natural language processing, and fraud detection.

Prediction and Classification: Machine learning algorithms are often used for prediction and classification tasks. By learning from historical data, these algorithms can make predictions about future outcomes or classify new data points into predefined categories. Common examples include predicting stock prices, classifying emails as spam or not, and diagnosing medical conditions.

Optimization: Algorithms are employed to optimize processes and make them more efficient. For example, optimization algorithms can be used to find the best route for delivery vehicles, allocate resources effectively, or fine-tune parameters in a machine learning model for improved performance.

Automation of Decision-Making: In various domains, algorithms automate decision-making processes. This is evident in recommendation systems that suggest products, movies, or content based on user preferences, as well as in automated trading systems that make buy or sell decisions in financial markets.

Clustering and Segmentation: Algorithms are utilized for clustering and segmenting data into groups with similar characteristics. This is valuable for market segmentation, customer profiling, and other applications where identifying distinct groups within a dataset is beneficial.

Learning from Data: Machine learning algorithms, a subset of algorithms, have the capacity to learn from data. They improve their performance over time by adjusting their internal parameters based on the patterns and relationships observed in the training data. This enables them to make more accurate predictions on new, unseen data.

Data Transformation: Algorithms are used to transform data into different representations or formats. For instance, dimensionality reduction algorithms like Principal Component Analysis (PCA) transform high-dimensional data into a lower-dimensional space while retaining essential information.

Solving Complex Problems: Algorithms are essential for solving complex computational problems that may involve intricate mathematical calculations, simulations, or optimizations. They are the core tools used to address a wide range of challenges in science, engineering, and business.

Understanding the role of algorithms involves recognizing their versatility in solving diverse problems and their ability to handle complex computations and decision-making tasks. The selection of the appropriate algorithm is crucial and depends on the specific nature of the problem at hand, the characteristics of the data, and the desired outcomes.

4.5 Choosing the Right Algorithm:

The choice of algorithm can significantly impact the model's performance. We discuss considerations for selecting algorithms based on the nature of the task, the characteristics of the data, and the desired outcome.

Choosing the right algorithm is a crucial decision in any data science or machine learning project, as it significantly influences the model's performance and the outcomes of the analysis. Here are key considerations to guide the process of selecting the appropriate algorithm:

Understand the Problem Type: Clearly define the problem you are trying to solve: Is it a classification, regression, clustering, or another type of problem? The nature of your problem will guide the choice of algorithms designed for specific tasks.

Consider the Size and Nature of the Data: Assess the characteristics of your dataset, including its size, dimensionality, and the type of features it contains. Some algorithms perform better with large datasets, while others are more suitable for high-dimensional or sparse data.

Evaluate Computational Complexity: Consider the computational resources required by different algorithms. Some algorithms are computationally more intensive and may not be suitable for large-scale datasets or real-time applications.

Check for Linearity: Determine if the relationships in your data are linear or non-linear. Linear models like linear regression or support vector machines are suitable for linear relationships, while non-linear models like decision trees or neural networks may capture more complex patterns.

Examine Model Interpretability: Assess the interpretability of the model. Some algorithms, like decision trees or linear models, provide easily interpretable results, which can be important for understanding and explaining the model's predictions.

Handle Imbalanced Data: If your dataset has imbalanced classes, where one class significantly outnumbers the others, choose algorithms that handle imbalanced data well. Some algorithms may require specific techniques or adjustments to address class imbalance effectively.

Consider Robustness to Outliers: Evaluate the robustness of algorithms to outliers in your data. Some algorithms, like decision trees, can handle outliers naturally, while others, like linear regression, may be sensitive to extreme values.

Assess Feature Importance: If understanding feature importance is crucial, consider algorithms that provide insights into feature importance. Decision trees and ensemble methods like Random Forest are known for their ability to highlight important features.

Account for Model Complexity: Balance the complexity of the model with the amount of available data. Overly complex models may lead to overfitting, especially with limited data, while overly simple models may underfit and fail to capture the underlying patterns.

Explore Ensemble Methods: Ensemble methods, such as Random Forests or Gradient Boosting, can often improve predictive performance by combining the strengths of multiple models. They are robust and can handle various types of data.

Validate and Iterate: Experiment with different algorithms and evaluate their performance using cross-validation. Iterate and refine your choice based on the results, continuously assessing whether the selected algorithm aligns with the goals of your project.

Choosing the right algorithm involves a combination of domain knowledge, experimentation, and a deep understanding of the characteristics of your data. It's often beneficial to try multiple algorithms and compare their performance to ensure that the chosen model is well-suited for the specific task at hand.

4.6 Training and Testing Data:

Splitting data into training and testing sets is crucial for assessing how well the model generalizes to new, unseen data. We explore best practices for this division, avoiding common pitfalls that may lead to overfitting or underfitting.

In the context of machine learning, the use of training and testing data is a fundamental practice to assess the performance and generalization capabilities of a model. Here's an explanation of these concepts:

Training Data:

Definition: Training data is the portion of the dataset used to train or teach the machine learning model. It consists of input-output pairs, where the input represents the features or attributes, and the output is the corresponding target or label. The model learns patterns, relationships, and associations from this data to make predictions or classifications.

Purpose: The primary goal of training data is to enable the model to learn the underlying patterns in the data. During the training phase, the model adjusts its parameters iteratively to minimize the difference between its predictions and the actual outcomes in the training set.

Testing Data:

Definition: Testing data, also referred to as a test set or validation set, is a separate portion of the dataset that is not used during the training phase. It serves as an unseen dataset against which the model's performance is evaluated after training.

Purpose: The purpose of testing data is to assess how well the model generalizes to new, previously unseen data. By evaluating the model on data it has not encountered during training, one can estimate its performance on real-world scenarios and detect potential issues like overfitting (where the model memorizes the training data but performs poorly on new data).

Training-Testing Split:

Methodology: The dataset is typically divided into two parts: a training set and a testing set. Common split ratios include 70-30, 80-20, or 90-10, where the larger portion is used for training, and the smaller portion is reserved for testing. Randomization is often applied to ensure a representative distribution of data in both sets.

Best Practices: It is essential to maintain the independence of the training and testing sets. Once the model is trained, it should not see or have access to the testing data until the evaluation phase to ensure an unbiased assessment of its generalization performance.

Cross-Validation:

Extension: In addition to a simple training-testing split, cross-validation is a technique that involves multiple rounds of splitting the data into training and testing sets. This helps provide a more robust estimate of the model's performance by averaging results over different partitions of the data.

The use of training and testing data is critical for building reliable and effective machine learning models. It allows practitioners to gauge how well a model is likely to perform on new, unseen data, which is a key factor in assessing its real-world utility. Properly managing and partitioning data into training and testing sets is a foundational step in the machine learning workflow.

4.7 Model Evaluation Metrics:

How do we measure the success of a machine learning model? This section introduces various evaluation metrics, such as accuracy, precision, recall, and F1 score. Understanding these metrics is essential for gauging how well your model performs on different tasks.

Model evaluation metrics are measures used to assess the performance of machine learning models. The choice of metrics depends on the nature of the problem (classification, regression, clustering, etc.) and the specific goals of the analysis. Here are common model evaluation metrics for different types of tasks:

<u>Classification Metrics:</u>

Accuracy:

Definition: Proportion of correctly classified instances among the total instances.

Use Case: Suitable for balanced datasets; however, it can be misleading in imbalanced datasets.

Precision:

Definition: Proportion of true positive predictions among all positive predictions.

Use Case: Important when minimizing false positives is critical.

Recall (Sensitivity or True Positive Rate):

Definition: Proportion of true positive predictions among all actual positive instances.

Use Case: Important when identifying all positive instances is crucial.

F1 Score:

Definition: Harmonic mean of precision and recall, balancing both metrics.

Use Case: Useful when there's a need to balance precision and recall.

Area Under the Receiver Operating Characteristic (ROC-AUC):

Definition: Area under the ROC curve, which plots the true positive rate against the false positive rate.

Use Case: Applicable to binary classification problems, particularly when the balance between sensitivity and specificity is important.

Confusion Matrix:

Definition: A table representing the count of true positive, true negative, false positive, and false negative predictions.

Use Case: Provides a detailed breakdown of model performance.

<u>**Regression Metrics:**</u>

Mean Squared Error (MSE):

Definition: Average of the squared differences between predicted and actual values.

Use Case: Sensitive to outliers; penalizes larger errors heavily.

Mean Absolute Error (MAE):

Definition: Average of the absolute differences between predicted and actual values.

Use Case: Less sensitive to outliers compared to MSE.

R-squared (Coefficient of Determination):

Definition: Proportion of the variance in the dependent variable explained by the model.

Use Case: Indicates the goodness of fit; ranges from 0 to 1.

<u>**Clustering Metrics:**</u>

Silhouette Score:

Definition: Measures how well-separated clusters are. Ranges from -1 (incorrect clustering) to 1 (well-separated clusters).

Use Case: Assessing the quality of clustering.

Davies-Bouldin Index:

Definition: Measures the compactness and separation of clusters. Lower values indicate better clustering.

Use Case Evaluating the quality of clusters.

<u>Common Metrics for Imbalanced Datasets:</u>

Precision-Recall Curve:

Definition: A curve that represents the trade-off between precision and recall for different threshold values.

Use Case: Particularly useful in imbalanced datasets where the positive class is rare.

Area Under the Precision-Recall Curve (PR AUC):**

Definition: Area under the precision-recall curve.

Use Case: Quantifies the model's performance across different precision-recall trade-offs.

Choosing the appropriate metric depends on the goals of the analysis and the specific challenges posed by the task at hand. It's often advisable to consider multiple metrics to gain a comprehensive understanding of a model's performance.

In the subsequent chapters, we delve into specific supervised and unsupervised learning techniques, exploring their applications, strengths, and limitations. From linear regression to advanced neural networks, you'll gain a comprehensive understanding of the diverse set of tools at your disposal in the realm of machine learning. Stay tuned for a deep dive into the intricacies of each technique and practical tips for implementation.

Chapter 5.0 Supervised Learning Techniques:

Supervised learning is a type of machine learning where the algorithm is trained on a labelled dataset, meaning that the input data is paired with corresponding output labels. The goal of supervised learning is for the algorithm to learn a mapping from inputs to outputs, enabling it to make predictions or decisions when given new, unseen data. Here are some common supervised learning techniques:

This chapter is a gateway to the fascinating world of supervised learning, where models are trained on labelled datasets to make predictions or classifications. We will explore various techniques, each with its unique strengths and applications, offering you a diverse toolkit for solving a wide range of problems.

5.1 Linear Regression:

Linear regression is the bedrock of regression analysis. It models the relationship between a dependent variable and one or more independent variables by fitting a linear equation to observed data. In this section, we'll delve into the mathematics behind linear regression, explore its applications, and guide you through implementing it for predictive tasks.

Linear Regression is a supervised learning algorithm used for predicting a continuous target variable based on one or more predictor features. The fundamental assumption is that there exists a linear relationship between the input features and the target variable. The algorithm aims to find the best-fitting line (or hyperplane in higher dimensions) that minimizes the sum of squared differences between the predicted and actual values.

Mathematical Representation:

For a simple linear regression with one predictor variable:

$$y = \beta 0 + \beta 1 . x + \varepsilon$$

Where...

y is the target variable.

x is the predictor variable.

$\beta 0$ is the y-intercept (constant term).

$\beta 1$ is the slope of the line.

ε represents the error term (the difference between the predicted and actual values).

For multiple linear regression with n predictor variables:

$$y = \beta 0 + \beta 1 . x1 + \beta 2 . x2 \ldots\ldots\ldots \beta n . xn + \varepsilon$$

Example:

Let's consider a simple example where we want to predict the price of a house (y) based on its size in square feet (x). We assume a linear relationship between the size of the house and its price.

Data Collection: Gather a dataset with information on house sizes and their corresponding prices.

Data Exploration: Plot a scatter plot of house size (x) versus price (y) to visually inspect the relationship.

Model Training:1

Use linear regression to find the best-fitting line. The model estimates the values of $\beta 0$ and $\beta 1$) that minimize the sum of squared differences between predicted and actual prices.

Model Representation:

The linear regression model can be represented as Price $= \beta 0 + \beta 1$. Size $+ \varepsilon$.

Model Evaluation:

Assess the model's performance using evaluation metrics such as Mean Squared Error (MSE) or R-squared. These metrics quantify the accuracy and goodness of fit of the model.

Prediction:

Use the trained model to predict the price of a new house given its size.

Python Example using Scikit-Learn:

Python

import numpy as np

from sklearn.linear_model import LinearRegression

import matplotlib.pyplot as plt

Sample data

size = np.array([1400, 1600, 1700, 1875, 1100, 1550, 2350, 2450, 1425, 1700])

price = np.array([245000, 312000, 279000, 308000, 199000, 219000, 405000, 324000, 319000, 255000])

Reshape the data for Scikit-Learn

X = size.reshape(-1, 1)

y = price

Create and train the linear regression model

```
model = LinearRegression()
model.fit(X, y)
```

Make predictions

```
new_size = np.array([2000]).reshape(-1, 1)
predicted_price = model.predict(new_size)
Plot the data and the regression line
plt.scatter(size, price, label='Actual Data')
plt.plot(size, model.predict(X), color='red', label='Linear Regression')
plt.scatter(new_size, predicted_price, color='green', marker='X', label='Predicted Price')
plt.xlabel('House Size (sq. ft)')
plt.ylabel('Price')
plt.title('Linear Regression Example')
plt.legend()
plt.show()
print(f"Predicted Price for a house with size 2000 sq. ft: ${predicted_price[0]:,.2f}")
```

This example demonstrates the application of linear regression to predict house prices based on their sizes. The model finds the best-fitting line that represents the relationship between house size and price, allowing for predictions on new data points.

5.2 Decision Trees and Random Forests:

Decision trees are intuitive models that mimic human decision-making processes. We'll discuss how decision trees work, explore the concept of splitting nodes, and delve into the potential issues like overfitting. Random Forests, an ensemble of decision trees, will be introduced as a powerful technique for improving model performance and robustness.

Decision Trees:

A Decision Tree is a supervised machine learning algorithm used for both classification and regression tasks. It works by recursively splitting the dataset into subsets based on the most significant attribute at each level, creating a tree-like structure. The decision-making process involves evaluating conditions along the branches of the tree until a final decision or prediction is reached at the leaf nodes.

Node Splitting: At each node, the algorithm selects the feature that best separates the data, based on criteria such as Gini impurity (for classification) or mean squared error (for regression). The chosen feature becomes the decision node, and the dataset is split into subsets accordingly.

Leaf Nodes: The process continues until a stopping criterion is met, such as reaching a predetermined depth or having a minimum number of samples in a node. The terminal nodes are called leaf nodes, and they represent the final predictions or classifications.

Advantages of Decision Trees:

- Intuitive and easy to interpret, mimicking human decision-making.
- Requires minimal data preprocessing (e.g., no need for feature scaling).
- Handles both numerical and categorical data.

Disadvantages and Considerations:

- Prone to overfitting, especially with deep trees.
- Can be sensitive to noisy data.
- Lack of robustness; small changes in data can lead to different tree structures.

Random Forests:

A Random Forest is an ensemble learning method that builds multiple decision trees and combines their predictions to improve accuracy and generalization. Each tree in the forest is constructed independently, often with a random subset of features and a bootstrapped sample of the training data.

Bootstrap Sampling: Random Forest uses bootstrapped sampling, meaning that each tree is trained on a subset of the original data formed by randomly selecting samples with replacement.

Feature Randomization: At each node of the decision tree, a random subset of features is considered for splitting. This helps decorrelate the trees and prevents a dominant feature from overpowering the ensemble.

Voting or Averaging: In classification tasks, the final prediction is often determined by a majority vote among the trees. In regression tasks, it may involve averaging the predictions.

Advantages of Random Forests:

- Mitigates overfitting by combining multiple trees.
- Provides feature importance rankings.
- Robust performance across diverse datasets.

Disadvantages and Considerations:

- Increased complexity compared to individual decision trees.
- Computational cost may be higher due to the ensemble

structure.
- May not be as easily interpretable as a single decision tree.

To make it very clear, let us take an Example:

Suppose you want to predict whether a customer will purchase a product based on features like age, income, and browsing history. A decision tree might start by evaluating the age feature, determining a threshold, and splitting the data into two subsets (e.g., younger and older customers). The process continues recursively, leading to a tree structure with decision nodes and leaf nodes. A Random Forest would involve creating multiple such trees, each trained on a different subset of the data and potentially considering different subsets of features at each node. The ensemble then combines the predictions to yield a more robust and accurate result.

5.3 Support Vector Machines:

Support Vector Machines (SVM) are versatile algorithms used for both classification and regression tasks. We'll explore the mathematical foundations of SVM, understand the concept of hyperplanes, and discuss how kernel functions can be employed to handle non-linear relationships in data.

Support Vector Machines (SVM) is a supervised machine learning algorithm used for both classification and regression tasks. It is particularly effective in scenarios where a clear margin of separation between classes is sought. The primary objective of SVM is to find the hyperplane that best separates data points of different classes while maximizing the margin between the classes.

Key Concepts:

Hyperplane: In SVM, a hyperplane is a decision boundary that separates the data points of one class from another. For two-dimensional data, a hyperplane is a line; for three-dimensional data, it's a plane, and so on. In higher dimensions, it becomes a hyperplane.

Margin: The margin is the distance between the hyperplane and the nearest data point from either class. SVM aims to find the hyperplane that maximizes this margin. A larger margin is desirable as it reflects a more robust and generalizable separation between classes.

Support Vectors: Support vectors are the data points that lie closest to the hyperplane and play a crucial role in determining the optimal hyperplane. These are the points that, if moved or removed, could change the position of the hyperplane.

Kernel Trick: SVM can efficiently handle non-linear decision boundaries by transforming the input features into a higher-dimensional space. The kernel trick allows the algorithm to compute the decision boundary in this higher-dimensional space without explicitly calculating the transformed feature vectors.

<u>**Working of SVM:**</u>

Input Data: Given a dataset with labelled instances belonging to different classes, SVM aims to find the hyperplane that best separates these classes.

Feature Transformation (Kernel Trick): If the data is not linearly separable in the original feature space, SVM can use a kernel function to map the data into a higher-dimensional space where a hyperplane can be used for separation.

Optimizing the Hyperplane: SVM seeks to find the hyperplane that maximizes the margin between classes. This is done by solving a constrained optimization problem, where the goal is to minimize the norm of the weight vector subject to the constraint that all data points are correctly classified and lie on the correct side of the hyperplane.

Classification: Once the optimal hyperplane is determined, new data points can be classified based on which side of the hyperplane they fall.

<u>**Types of SVM:**</u>

C-Support Vector Classification (C-SVC): This is the standard form of SVM for classification tasks. The parameter C controls the trade-off between achieving a low training error and a large margin.

Nu-Support Vector Classification (Nu-SVC): Similar to C-SVC, but uses a parameter ν to control the number of support vectors and training errors. It provides a different way of controlling the trade-off between error and margin.

Epsilon-Support Vector Regression (epsilon-SVR): SVM can also be used for regression tasks, where it tries to fit the best hyperplane within a margin of ϵ around the actual values.

Example:

Consider a dataset with two classes of data points, red circles, and blue squares, scattered in two-dimensional space. SVM seeks to find the hyperplane that maximizes the margin between these two classes.

The optimal hyperplane is the one that ensures the maximum separation between the support vectors of the two classes. In the case of non-linearly separable data, a kernel function can be employed to transform the data into a higher-dimensional space, making it possible to find a hyperplane that separates the classes effectively. The choice of kernel (e.g., linear, polynomial, radial basis function) depends on the characteristics of the data and the problem at hand.

5.4 Neural Networks:

Neural networks are the backbone of deep learning. We'll start with the basics, understanding the structure of neural networks, the role of layers and neurons, and the process of forward and backward propagation. This section provides a stepping stone for more advanced topics, such as convolutional neural networks (CNNs) and recurrent neural networks (RNNs).

Each supervised learning technique will be accompanied by practical examples, code snippets, and considerations for selecting the right algorithm based on the characteristics of your data and the nature of your task.

Neural Networks:

A Nural Network is a powerful and versatile machine learning model inspired by the structure and functioning of the human brain. It consists of interconnected nodes, called neurons, organized into layers. Neural networks are used for a wide range of tasks, including classification, regression, pattern recognition, and more complex tasks like natural language processing and image recognition.

Key Components:

<u>Neurons:</u>

Neurons are the basic building blocks of a neural network. Each neuron receives input, performs a computation, and produces an output. The inputs are multiplied by weights, summed, and passed through an activation function to produce the neuron's output.

<u>Layers:</u>

A neural network is organized into layers. The most common layers are:

Input Layer: Receives the initial input data.

Hidden Layers: Intermediate layers between the input and output layers. These layers contribute to the model's ability to learn complex patterns.

Output Layer: Produces the final output of the network.

<u>Weights and Biases:</u>

Weights represent the strength of connections between neurons, determining the impact of one neuron's output on another. Biases are added to the weighted sum before passing through the activation function, allowing the network to learn more complex relationships.

<u>Activation Functions:</u>

Activation functions introduce non-linearity into the network, enabling it to learn and approximate complex, non-linear relationships in data. Common activation functions include sigmoid, tanh, and rectified linear unit (ReLU).

<u>Loss Function:</u>

The loss function measures the difference between the predicted output and the actual target. The goal during training is to minimize this loss, adjusting the weights and biases to improve the model's predictions.

<u>Optimization Algorithm:</u>

Optimization algorithms, like gradient descent, are used to minimize the loss function by iteratively adjusting the weights and biases. The gradient of the loss with respect to the parameters guides the updates.

Training Process:

<u>Forward Propagation:</u>

The input data is passed through the network, layer by layer, using the current weights and biases. The output is generated, and the loss is computed.

<u>Backward Propagation:</u>

The gradients of the loss with respect to the weights and biases are computed through backpropagation. This involves computing the error contribution of each weight and adjusting them accordingly.

<u>Weight Update:</u>

The weights and biases are updated using an optimization algorithm (e.g., gradient descent) to minimize the loss. This process is repeated iteratively until the model converges to a satisfactory solution.

Types of Neural Networks:

Feedforward Neural Networks (FNN): The most basic type of neural network where information travels in one direction—from input to output.

Recurrent Neural Networks (RNN): Designed to work with sequences of data, RNNs have connections that form directed cycles, allowing them to maintain a memory of previous inputs.

Convolutional Neural Networks (CNN): Specialized for processing grid-like data, such as images. CNNs use convolutional layers to automatically and adaptively learn spatial hierarchies of features.

Generative Adversarial Networks (GAN): Comprises a generator and a discriminator. The generator creates data, and the discriminator evaluates it. They are trained together in a competitive setting, leading to the generation of realistic data.

Example:

Consider a simple feedforward neural network for image classification. The network has an input layer, one or more hidden layers, and an output layer. Each neuron in the input layer represents a pixel of the input image. The hidden layers and output layer contain neurons with weights and biases learned during training.

```
import tensorflow as tf
from tensorflow.keras import layers, models
Define a simple neural network
model = models.Sequential([
layers.Flatten(input_shape=(28, 28)), # Flatten 2D input to 1D
layers.Dense(128, activation='relu'), # Hidden layer with ReLU activation
```

layers.Dense(10, activation='softmax') # Output layer with softmax activation for classification
])

Compile the model with a loss function, optimizer, and evaluation metric

model.compile(optimizer='adam',
loss='sparse_categorical_crossentropy',
metrics=['accuracy'])

Display the model architecture

model.summary()

In this example, we use TensorFlow and Keras to create a simple feedforward neural network for image classification. The model is defined with a flattening layer to convert the 2D input image into a 1D vector, a hidden layer with ReLU activation, and an output layer with softmax activation for classification. The model is then compiled with a specified loss function, optimizer, and evaluation metric. During training, the weights and biases are adjusted to minimize the specified loss, resulting in a model capable of making accurate predictions on new data.

Chapter 6.0 Unsupervised Learning Techniques:

While supervised learning deals with labelled data, unsupervised learning dives into the unknown, seeking patterns and structures in unlabelled datasets.

In simple terms, Unsupervised learning is a machine learning paradigm where the algorithm is tasked with extracting patterns or relationships from a dataset without explicit guidance or labelled examples. In other words, the algorithm explores the data on its own, identifying inherent structures, similarities, or anomalies without being told what to look for. This contrasts with supervised learning, where the algorithm is trained on labelled data with explicit input-output pairs. Unsupervised learning is particularly useful for tasks such as clustering similar data points, reducing the dimensionality of complex datasets, and detecting anomalies or unusual patterns within the data.

This chapter explores the power of unsupervised learning techniques in uncovering hidden insights and relationships.

Clustering: K-Means and Hierarchical

Clustering is a fundamental unsupervised learning technique, aiming to group similar data points together. We'll explore K-Means clustering, a centroid-based method, and Hierarchical clustering, which builds a tree of clusters. Practical applications and considerations for choosing the right clustering method will be discussed.

6.1 K-Means Clustering and Hierarchical

<u>K-Means Clustering</u>

✓ K-Means is like organizing items into K number of groups (clusters), where K is a predefined number.

✓ For example, imagine you have a dataset of customer purchases, and you want to group them based on their buying behavior. K-Means would separate them into K clusters based on similarities in their purchase patterns.

✓ The algorithm starts by randomly assigning K cluster centers and then iteratively adjusts them to minimize the distance between data points and their assigned cluster center.

✓ The result is that similar data points end up in the same cluster.

Example: Consider a dataset of customer spending on clothing and electronics. K-Means might identify two clusters - one for customers who spend more on clothing and another for those who spend more on electronics.

<u>Hierarchical Clustering:</u>

✓ Hierarchical clustering builds a tree-like structure of clusters. It doesn't require specifying the number of clusters beforehand.

✓ Imagine you have a dataset of animals, and you want to group them hierarchically based on features like habitat, diet, etc.

✓ The algorithm starts by treating each data point as a single cluster and then merges the closest clusters until there is only one cluster left.

✓ The resulting tree, called a dendrogram, allows you to choose the number of clusters by cutting it at a certain height.

Example: In the animal dataset, hierarchical clustering might show that initially, reptiles and amphibians are separate clusters, but as the tree progresses, they eventually merge into a broader category of "cold-blooded animals."

6.2. Dimensionality Reduction: Principal Component Analysis (PCA)

PCA is a technique used to reduce the number of features (dimensions) in a dataset while retaining its essential information.

✓ PCA identifies the directions (principal components) in which the data varies the most and projects the data onto these components.

✓ For example, if you have a dataset with information about a car's speed, weight, fuel efficiency, etc., PCA might identify that most of the variability comes from a combination of speed and weight, allowing you to represent the data in a simpler way.

Example: In a dataset with information about a car's features, PCA might reveal that speed and weight are the most critical factors. So, instead of using all the original features, you can represent each car by its speed and weight, simplifying the dataset.

6.3. Anomaly Detection

Anomaly detection involves identifying unusual patterns or data points in a dataset that don't conform to the expected behaviour. Anomaly detection is crucial in various fields, such as fraud detection, network security, and industrial quality control.

Example: Consider a network traffic dataset. Most of the time, the data reflects normal user behaviour. Anomaly detection algorithms can identify unusual patterns that might indicate a potential security threat, like a hacker attempting to breach the system.

In conclusion, unsupervised learning techniques, including clustering, dimensionality reduction, and anomaly detection, provide valuable tools for exploring and understanding complex datasets without explicit guidance. Whether it's grouping similar data points, simplifying information, or identifying unusual patterns, these techniques play a crucial role in extracting meaningful insights from unlabelled data.

Chapter 7.0 Introduction to Deep Learning:

Deep learning is a subset of machine learning that involves the use of artificial neural networks to model and solve complex problems. These neural networks are inspired by the structure and function of the human brain, consisting of interconnected layers of nodes (artificial neurons). The term "deep" in deep learning refers to the depth of these neural networks, indicating the presence of multiple layers between the input and output layers.

7.1 Importance of Deep Learning:

Deep learning is crucial for advancing artificial intelligence and machine learning due to its unparalleled ability to automatically learn complex hierarchical representations from data. The significance of deep learning lies in its capacity to handle intricate patterns and relationships within large datasets, enabling breakthroughs in tasks such as image and speech recognition, natural language processing, and computer vision.

The depth of neural networks allows for feature representation learning, where lower layers capture simpler features and higher layers combine them to represent more abstract concepts. This end-to-end learning approach, coupled with advancements in handling big data, positions deep learning as a transformative force, powering innovations across various domains and setting new benchmarks in the development of intelligent system.

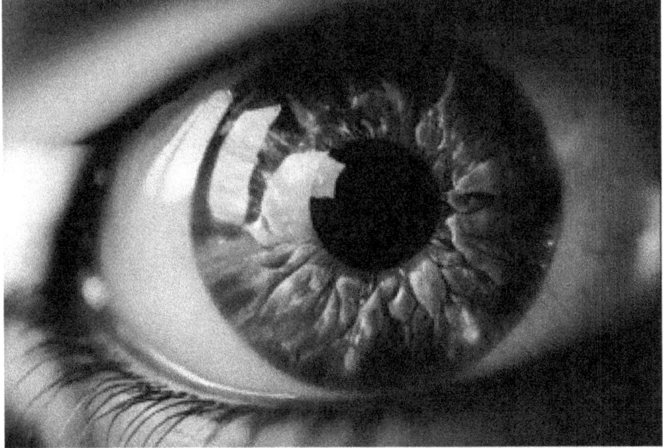

In this chapter, we venture into the transformative realm of deep learning, a subfield of machine learning that has witnessed unprecedented success in various applications.

From the basics of neural networks to advanced architectures like Convolutional Neural Networks (CNNs) and Recurrent Neural

Networks (RNNs), this chapter is your gateway to understanding the power and complexity of deep learning.

7.2 Neural Networks Basics:

We begin with the foundational concepts of neural networks. Understanding the structure of neurons, activation functions, and the flow of information through layers is crucial. This section also introduces the concept of training neural networks using backpropagation, the optimization process, and the role of loss functions.

Neural Networks Overview:

Neural networks are a class of machine learning models inspired by the structure and function of the human brain. They are used for tasks such as pattern recognition, classification, regression, and more. The basic building block of a neural network is the neuron, and these neurons are organized into layers.

Neurons and Layers:

Neurons:

✓ A neuron takes input, processes it, and produces an output.

✓ It has weights that adjust during training, representing the strength of connections between neurons.

✓ The output of a neuron is often passed through an activation function, which introduces non-linearity to the model.

Layers:

✓ Neurons are organized into layers. The three main types of layers are:

✓ Input Layer: The first layer that receives the initial input data.

✓ Hidden Layers: Layers between the input and output layers where computations occur.

✓ Output Layer: Produces the final output.

Neural Network Example:

Let's consider a simple example of a neural network for binary classification (distinguishing between two classes).

Input:

Suppose we want to predict whether a student will pass (1) or fail (0) based on the number of hours they study.

Architecture:

✓ One input layer with a single neuron (as we have only one feature - hours of study).

✓ One hidden layer with, let's say, three neurons.

✓ One output layer with a single neuron (as we want a binary output).

Connections:

Each connection between neurons has a weight, representing the importance of that connection.

Training:

During training, the network learns by adjusting the weights based on the error between predicted and actual outcomes.

Forward Pass:

✓ The number of hours studied is the input to the input layer.

✓ The input is multiplied by weights and passed through an activation function in the hidden layer.

✓ The output of the hidden layer is then multiplied by another set of weights and passed through an activation function to produce the final prediction.

Backward Pass (Training):

The difference between the predicted and actual outcomes (error) is used to adjust the weights backward through the network, using a process called backpropagation.

Activation Function:

Common choices include the sigmoid function for the output layer in binary classification.

This is a basic example, and neural networks can become much more complex with more layers, neurons, and types of connections. But the fundamental principles remain the same: learning from data by adjusting weights to make accurate predictions.

7.3 Convolutional Neural Networks (CNN):

Convolutional Neural Networks CNNs have revolutionized image processing and pattern recognition. We explore the architecture of CNNs, including convolutional layers, pooling layers, and fully connected layers. Applications of CNNs in image classification, object detection, and image generation will be elucidated through practical examples.

CNNs are a class of deep neural networks specifically designed for tasks involving images and spatial data. They are particularly good at capturing patterns and spatial hierarchies in data.

Key Components:
Convolutional Layers:

✓ These layers use filters (small windows) to scan across the input data.

✓ Each filter detects specific features like edges, textures, or more complex patterns.

✓ Convolution involves element-wise multiplication and summation of the filter and local regions of the input.

Pooling Layers:

✓ After convolution, pooling layers are often applied to downsample the spatial dimensions.

✓ Common pooling operations include max pooling (selecting the maximum value in a region) or average pooling (taking the average).

Fully Connected Layers:

✓ After several convolutional and pooling layers, the high-level reasoning is captured in the final layers.

✓ These layers are typically fully connected, similar to traditional neural networks.

Example: Detecting Digits in Images

To explain it in a simple way, let's say we want to build a CNN to recognize handwritten digits (like the digits 0-9).

Architecture:

Input Layer:

For simplicity, let's assume our input is a grayscale image of size 28x28 pixels.

Convolutional Layers:

We apply several convolutional layers with different filters. These filters might detect simple patterns like edges in the early layers and more complex patterns like loops or intersections in deeper layers.

Pooling Layers:

After each convolutional layer, we add pooling layers to reduce spatial dimensions and focus on the most important features.

Flattening:

The output of the convolutional and pooling layers is then flattened into a vector.

Fully Connected Layers:

We add fully connected layers at the end to make predictions. Each neuron in the final layer represents the likelihood of a specific digit (0-9).

Training:

✓ During training, the network adjusts its weights using labeled data (images with known digit labels).

✓ The convolutional layers learn to extract features, and the fully connected layers learn to classify based on these features.

Forward Pass:

✓ An input image goes through the convolutional layers, pooling layers, and fully connected layers.

✓ The final layer produces a probability distribution over the possible digits.

Backward Pass (Training):

The difference between the predicted probabilities and the actual labels is used to adjust the weights using backpropagation.

In this way, the CNN learns to recognize patterns and features in the images, making it capable of accurately classifying handwritten digits.

7.4 Recurrent Neural Networks (RNN):

RNNs are designed to handle sequential data, making them invaluable for tasks such as natural language processing and time-series analysis. We delve into the structure of RNNs, recurrent connections, and the challenges of long-term dependencies. Practical applications include text generation, language translation, and predicting time-series data.

Recurrent Neural Networks (RNNs) are a type of neural network designed for sequences of data, making them suitable for tasks like natural language processing, time series analysis, and more. Unlike feedforward neural networks, RNNs have connections that create loops, allowing information to persist.

<u>Key Concepts:</u>

Sequential Data:

RNNs are excellent for handling sequences, where the order of data points matters. Examples include time series data, sentences, or musical notes.

Recurrent Connections:

✓ The key feature of RNNs is the presence of recurrent connections, which allow information to be passed from one step of the sequence to the next.

✓ This enables the network to maintain a memory of previous inputs, making it well-suited for tasks with temporal dependencies.

Example: Language Modelling

Let's use a simple example of an RNN for language modeling. Suppose we want to predict the next word in a sentence based on the preceding words.

Architecture:

Input Layer:

Each word in the sequence is represented as a vector and fed into the network one at a time.

Recurrent Layer:

✓ The recurrent layer processes each word while maintaining an internal state that captures information about the previous words in the sequence.

✓ The internal state is updated at each time step, allowing the network to remember context.

Output Layer:

The final output layer produces a probability distribution over the vocabulary, indicating the likelihood of the next word.

Training:

✓ During training, the network learns to adjust its weights based on the error between predicted and actual next words.

✓ The recurrent connections allow the network to capture dependencies between words.

Forward Pass:

✓ The first word in the sequence is input to the network.

✓ The recurrent layer processes the word and updates its internal state.

✓ The updated state is used for predicting the probability distribution for the next word.

✓ This process repeats for each word in the sequence.

Backward Pass (Training):

The difference between the predicted and actual next words is used to adjust the weights, including the recurrent connections, using backpropagation through time.

In this way, an RNN can learn to model the structure and dependencies in sequences, making it useful for tasks such as language modeling, machine translation, and speech recognition. However, traditional RNNs have limitations in capturing long-term dependencies, leading to the development of more advanced models like Long Short-Term Memory (LSTM) and Gated Recurrent Unit (GRU). These variants address the vanishing gradient problem and enable more effective learning of long-range dependencies in sequential data.

7.5 Transfer Learning:

Transfer learning is a technique that leverages pre-trained models on large datasets for specific tasks. We discuss the advantages of transfer learning, explore popular pre-trained models, and guide you through the process of adapting these models to your specific applications.

As we journey through this chapter, you'll gain a comprehensive understanding of the architecture, training, and applications of neural networks. Deep learning opens up new possibilities for solving complex problems, and by the end of this chapter, you'll be equipped with the knowledge to embark on your own deep learning endeavours.

Transfer learning is a machine learning technique where a model trained on one task is adapted to perform a different but related task. The idea is to leverage the knowledge gained from solving one problem and apply it to a new, similar problem. Transfer learning is particularly useful when you have limited data for the task you want to perform.

Example: Image Classification with Pre-trained Models

Let's use image classification as an example:

Pre-training:

✓ Imagine you have a large dataset of images and you train a convolutional neural network (CNN) to recognize various objects in those images. This is your pre-trained model.

✓ The pre-trained model has learned to extract features and recognize patterns in images.

Transfer Learning:

✓ Now, you have a new, smaller dataset of images for a different task, let's say classifying specific breeds of dogs.

✓ Instead of training a new model from scratch on the small dataset (which might be challenging due to limited data), you use the pre-trained model as a starting point.

Adaptation:

✓ You take the pre-trained model and modify the last few layers or add new layers to it.

✓ The new layers are then trained on the smaller dataset specific to the dog breeds, while the weights of the pre-trained layers are kept frozen.

Fine-tuning:

You fine-tune the entire model on the new task, adjusting the weights of both the pre-trained layers and the newly added layers based on the new data.

You may ask what is the use of Transfer Learning. TL has got 3 important uses.

Advantages of Transfer Learning:

Knowledge Transfer: The pre-trained model has already learned useful features from a large dataset, which can be valuable for a new task.

Data Efficiency: Transfer learning allows you to achieve good performance on a new task even with a small amount of data.

Time Savings: Training a model from scratch on a new task can be time-consuming. Transfer learning helps in reducing the training time.

Note: Transfer learning is effective when the features learned from the source task are generalizable to the target task. It may not work well if the tasks are too dissimilar. For example, transferring knowledge from an image classification task to a text generation task might not be as effective as transferring between two image-related tasks.

Chapter 8.0 Model Deployment and Production:

Building a robust model is only the beginning; deploying it into real-world scenarios is the ultimate goal. This chapter guides you through the intricacies of model deployment, exploring methods to make your machine learning models accessible and operational in various environments.

Model Deployment: Model deployment is the process of taking a trained machine learning model and making it available for use in a real-world setting. It involves integrating the model into a production environment, allowing it to receive new input data, make predictions, and provide valuable outputs. Model deployment is a crucial step in the machine learning lifecycle, as it transitions a model from development and testing to practical use.

Production: In the context of machine learning, "production" refers to the live or operational environment where the model is actively making predictions or providing services based on real-time data. When a model is in production, it is actively used to handle tasks or problems for which it was designed. This could involve processing user requests, generating recommendations, classifying data, or any other task the model was trained to perform.

8.1 Exporting and Saving Models:

We discuss techniques for saving and exporting trained models in a format suitable for deployment. Whether it's a simple linear regression model or a complex neural network, understanding how to save and share your models is a crucial step.

Exporting and saving models refer to the process of preserving a trained machine learning model so that it can be used later for making predictions or sharing with others. Once a model is trained and tested, it's important to save its architecture, weights, and other relevant information for future use without having to retrain it.

The architecture of a model describes its structure, including the number and types of layers, connections between layers, and the type of activation functions used. Saving the architecture allows you to reconstruct the model later.

8.2 Web APIs for Machine Learning:

Integrating machine learning models into web applications requires the use of APIs (Application Programming Interfaces). This section explores the creation of web APIs for machine learning models, allowing seamless interaction between your models and external applications.

Web APIs (Application Programming Interfaces) for machine learning serve as a bridge between machine learning models and web applications. They enable developers to integrate machine learning capabilities seamlessly into web-based applications, allowing for real-time predictions, data processing, and other machine learning tasks. Here's an overview of key aspects related to web APIs for machine learning:

Endpoint for Inference:

The core function of a machine learning API is to provide an endpoint for making predictions (inference) based on input data. Clients (such as web applications) send requests to this endpoint with data, and the API responds with the model's predictions.

RESTful Architecture:

Many machine learning APIs follow a RESTful architecture, using HTTP methods (like GET or POST) for communication. RESTful APIs are stateless, scalable, and widely adopted, making them suitable for machine learning model deployment.

Data Formats:

APIs typically use standard data formats like JSON (JavaScript Object Notation) for exchanging data. Input data is sent as a request payload, and the model's predictions are returned as part of the response payload.

Authentication and Authorization:

To ensure secure access and prevent unauthorized use, machine learning APIs often implement authentication and authorization mechanisms. API keys, tokens, or other authentication methods may be required to access the API.

Scalability:

Web APIs for machine learning must be designed to handle varying levels of demand. Scalability considerations are crucial to ensure consistent and reliable performance, especially in production environments with multiple concurrent requests.

Error Handling:

Effective error handling is essential for a robust API. Clear and informative error messages help developers understand and address issues during integration or usage.

Model Versioning:

As machine learning models evolve, it's common to update or version them. API versioning allows developers to specify the version of the model they want to use, ensuring compatibility with their applications.

Documentation:

Comprehensive and well-maintained documentation is crucial for developers to understand how to interact with the API. This documentation typically includes details on endpoints, request formats, response formats, and any additional parameters.

Example: Using a Machine Learning API for Image Classification:

Endpoint:

The API provides an endpoint for image classification, allowing developers to send images for predictions.

Request Format:

Developers send a POST request to the API endpoint with an image file encoded in the request payload.

Authentication:

Authentication is handled using an API key, ensuring that only authorized users can access the service.

Response Format:

The API returns a JSON response containing the predicted class labels and associated probabilities for the input image.

Scalability:

The API is designed to handle a large number of concurrent requests, ensuring responsiveness even during peak usage.

Documentation:

The API documentation includes details on the endpoint, authentication, request format, and response format, helping developers integrate the image classification service into their applications.

Web APIs for machine learning play a pivotal role in bringing the power of machine learning models to a wide range of applications, from web and mobile apps to enterprise systems.

8.3 Considerations for Scalability:

Scalability is a key factor when deploying models in real-world scenarios. We discuss considerations for scaling your machine learning infrastructure, from handling large user loads to managing data storage and processing requirements.

Understanding how to deploy models effectively is very essential for translating machine learning concepts into tangible solutions. I have included all the typical points that are required for understanding **Scalability** in this chapter, as it bridges the gap between model development and real-world application, empowering you to bring your machine learning projects to life.

Scalability refers to the ability of a system to handle increasing amounts of work or demand efficiently. In the context of machine learning and web applications, scalability is a crucial consideration to ensure that the system can perform well under varying levels of load. Here are key considerations in my view for achieving scalability:

Horizontal vs. Vertical Scaling:

✓ Horizontal Scaling: Involves adding more machines or nodes to distribute the load. This is often achieved through technologies like load balancing, where incoming requests are distributed across multiple servers.

✓ Vertical Scaling: Involves increasing the resources (CPU, memory, etc.) of a single machine. While this approach has limits, it can be a quick solution for certain types of scaling needs.

Load Balancing:
Distributing incoming requests across multiple servers helps prevent a single server from becoming a bottleneck. Load balancers

can be implemented at different levels, such as application-level or network-level.

Caching:

Caching involves storing frequently accessed data in a temporary storage to reduce the need for repetitive computations or database queries. This can significantly improve response times and reduce the load on the system.

Asynchronous Processing:

Handling tasks asynchronously allows the system to continue processing requests without waiting for time-consuming operations to complete. This is especially useful for tasks like data processing, where results don't need to be instantly returned to the user.

Database Scalability:

Databases are often a common bottleneck. Consider strategies like database sharding (partitioning data across multiple databases), replication, or using distributed databases to scale horizontally.

Stateless Architecture:

Stateless applications don't store user state between requests, making it easier to scale horizontally by distributing requests to any available server. Session data can be stored externally (e.g., in a database) for persistence.

Microservices Architecture:

Breaking down a monolithic application into smaller, independent services (microservices) allows for independent scaling of different components. Each microservice can be deployed, updated, and scaled independently.

Cloud Services:

Cloud platforms offer scalable infrastructure and services. Leveraging cloud services allows dynamic allocation of resources based on demand, providing flexibility and cost efficiency.

Monitoring and Optimization:

Regularly monitor the performance of the system to identify bottlenecks or areas that need improvement. Optimization efforts should be data-driven and focused on improving the performance of critical components.

Auto-Scaling:

Auto-scaling allows the system to automatically adjust the number of resources based on demand. This can be particularly useful in cloud environments where resources can be dynamically provisioned or de-provisioned.

Failure Handling:

Design the system to gracefully handle failures. Redundancy, failover mechanisms, and proper error handling contribute to the system's overall resilience.

Scalable Algorithms:

For machine learning applications, choose algorithms that can scale with the size of the dataset. Some algorithms may become inefficient or impractical as data volumes increase.

Data Partitioning:

When dealing with large datasets, consider partitioning data based on relevant criteria. This allows for parallel processing and can enhance the scalability of data-intensive operations.

Scalability is a multifaceted consideration that involves architecture, infrastructure, and application design. Implementing scalable solutions is crucial for ensuring that systems can meet the growing demands while maintaining performance, reliability, and cost-effectiveness.

Stay tuned for the subsequent chapters, where we discuss the ethical considerations in machine learning and explore the future trends shaping this dynamic field.

Chapter 9.0 Ethical and Responsible Machine Learning:

As machine learning continues to permeate various aspects of our lives, ethical considerations become paramount requirement. In this chapter, we explore the ethical dimensions of machine learning, addressing issues such as bias, fairness, privacy, and accountability along with Industry guidelines and Best practices.

Ethical and responsible machine learning involves developing and deploying machine learning models in a manner that considers the broader impact on individuals, society, and the environment. It encompasses the principles of fairness, transparency, accountability, and the ethical treatment of data. Here are key aspects of ethical and responsible machine learning:

Fairness and Bias:

✓ **Issue**: Bias in training data or algorithms can lead to unfair treatment of certain individuals or groups, particularly in terms of race, gender, or socioeconomic status. Hence there should be absolutely No Bias in training data.

✓ **Mitigation**: Assess and address biases in training data, algorithms, and model outputs. Regularly monitor and evaluate models for fairness, and take corrective actions if bias is identified. This is more important, else if you fail to take corrective action by mitigation, it will directly reflet on your quality of output which will loose the trustworthiness.

Transparency:

✓ **Issue**: Lack of transparency in machine learning models can result in a lack of understanding about how decisions are made.

✓ **Mitigation**: Provide clear documentation on the model's objectives, training data, and decision-making process. Explainable AI techniques can help make complex models more understandable.

Accountability:

✓ **Issue**: When machine learning models make decisions that impact individuals or society, it's important to assign accountability.

✓ **Mitigation**: Clearly define roles and responsibilities. Establish mechanisms for accountability, and ensure that decision-makers can be held responsible for the consequences of model outputs.

Data Privacy:

✓ **Issue**: Improper handling of personal or sensitive data can lead to privacy violations.

✓ **Mitigation**: Implement robust data protection measures, anonymize or pseudonymize data when possible, and comply with relevant data protection regulations. Obtain informed consent when collecting and using personal data.

Informed Consent:

✓ **Issue**: Users may not be fully aware of how their data is being used or may not have given explicit consent.

✓ **Mitigation**: Clearly communicate how data will be used and seek explicit consent from individuals before collecting or processing their data. Provide options for users to opt-out if they wish.

Security:

✓ **Issue**: Inadequate security measures can lead to unauthorized access, data breaches, or malicious use of machine learning models.

✓ **Mitigation**: Implement strong security practices to protect models, data, and infrastructure. Regularly update and patch systems to address vulnerabilities.

Environmental Impact:

✓ Issue: Training large machine learning models can have a significant environmental impact due to high computational requirements.

✓ Mitigation: Consider energy-efficient algorithms, use renewable energy sources for computing infrastructure, and explore ways to minimize the carbon footprint of machine learning activities.

Societal Impact:

✓ **Issue**: Machine learning models can have unintended societal consequences, including job displacement or exacerbating existing social inequalities.

✓ **Mitigation**: Conduct thorough impact assessments before deploying models. Engage with diverse stakeholders, including impacted communities, to understand and address potential societal impacts.

Continuous Monitoring and Evaluation:

✓ **Issue**: Models can become outdated or exhibit unexpected behavior over time.

✓ **Mitigation**: Implement systems for continuous monitoring and evaluation of model performance. Regularly update models and retrain them with new, representative data.

Community Engagement:

✓ **Issue**: Lack of input from diverse perspectives in the development and deployment of machine learning models.

✓ **Mitigation**: Engage with a diverse set of stakeholders, including communities that may be affected by the models. Seek input, feedback, and collaboration to ensure a more inclusive decision-making process.

Industry Guidelines and Best Practices:

✓ Issue: Industry-specific considerations and practices can influence the fairness of machine learning applications. Certain industries may face unique ethical challenges or have specific best practices that need to be taken into account.

✓ Mitigation: Understand and adhere to industry-specific ethical guidelines and best practices. Engage with relevant industry organizations and communities to stay informed about emerging standards. Collaborate with peers to share knowledge and collectively address ethical challenges specific to the industry.

Ethical and responsible machine learning requires a holistic approach that involves not only technical considerations but also societal, legal, and environmental aspects. It involves an ongoing commitment to addressing ethical challenges and fostering a culture of responsibility within the machine learning community.

Various organizations and initiatives have developed guidelines and best practices for ethical machine learning. We provide an overview of these resources, including frameworks such as the Fairness, Accountability, and Transparency in Machine Learning (FAT/ML) principles and guidelines from leading organizations.

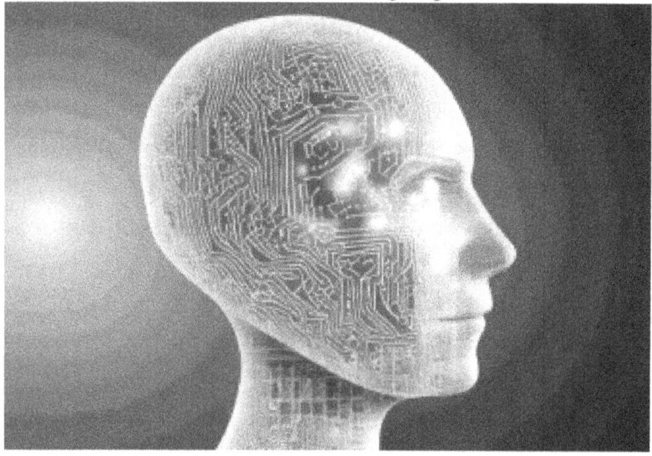

Navigating the ethical landscape of machine learning is crucial for building responsible and trustworthy systems. Hope after reading this Chapter, you would have a comprehensive understanding of the ethical challenges in machine learning and be equipped with tools and strategies to address them. As the field continues to evolve, ethical considerations will play an increasingly central role in shaping the responsible development and deployment of machine learning technologies.

Chapter 10.0 Future Trends in Machine Learning:

In this chapter, we embark on a forward-looking exploration of the emerging trends that are shaping the future of machine learning. From advancements in deep learning to the integration of machine learning with other cutting-edge technologies, this chapter provides insights into the potential developments of the field.

Predicting the future trends in Machine Learning involves some level of speculation, as AI is in its peak of developing more and more trendy explorations day by day. With several trends gaining momentum, here are some potential future trends in Machine Learning that I could able to figure out.

Explainable AI (XAI):

The demand for transparency and interpretability in machine learning models is increasing. Explainable AI aims to make complex models more understandable, especially in applications where decisions impact individuals or society.

Federated Learning:

Federated learning allows model training across decentralized devices or servers while keeping data localized. This approach addresses privacy concerns and enables collaborative model training without centralizing sensitive data.

AutoML and Automated Machine Learning Operations (MLOps):

Automated Machine Learning (AutoML) is evolving to streamline the entire machine learning lifecycle. MLOps focuses on automating the deployment, monitoring, and management of machine learning models, making the process more efficient.

AI Ethics and Responsible AI:

With increased awareness of ethical considerations, there is a growing emphasis on incorporating responsible AI practices. This includes addressing bias, ensuring fairness, and considering the broader societal impact of machine learning applications.

Edge AI:

Edge computing involves processing data closer to the source (e.g., on devices or at the network edge) rather than relying solely on centralized cloud servers. Edge AI brings machine learning capabilities to edge devices, enabling real-time processing and reducing latency.

Reinforcement Learning Advancements:

Reinforcement learning, a type of machine learning where agents learn by interacting with an environment, is seeing advancements. This includes applications in robotics, gaming, and decision-making systems.

AI in Healthcare:

Machine learning is expected to play a significant role in personalized medicine, drug discovery, diagnostics, and healthcare management. Predictive analytics and image recognition are among the areas where AI is making notable contributions.

Generative Adversarial Networks (GANs) Development:

GANs, which consist of two neural networks competing against each other, have shown promise in generating realistic content such as images, videos, and text. Future trends may involve further advancements in GANs' applications and capabilities.

Quantum Machine Learning:

As quantum computing technology progresses, the integration of quantum computing with machine learning algorithms is anticipated to bring new capabilities, particularly in solving complex optimization problems.

AI-driven Cybersecurity:

AI is increasingly being employed to enhance cybersecurity measures, identifying patterns, anomalies, and potential threats in real-time. Machine learning algorithms can adapt to evolving cyber threats and improve the overall security posture.

Human Augmentation with AI:

Future trends may include the integration of AI technologies to enhance human capabilities, ranging from improved decision-making support to physical augmentation, especially in areas like healthcare and industry.

Natural Language Processing (NLP) Advances:

Continued progress in natural language processing is expected, enabling more sophisticated language understanding, sentiment analysis, and language generation applications.

Advances in Deep Learning:

Deep learning is a dynamic field, and ongoing research continues to push its boundaries. This section explores recent and anticipated advancements in deep learning architectures, training techniques, and the application of deep learning to new domains. Topics may include unsupervised learning, self-supervised learning, and the development of more efficient and scalable models.

It's essential to note that the field of machine learning is dynamic, and new trends may emerge as technology advances and new challenges are addressed. Keeping abreast of the latest research and industry developments is crucial for staying informed about future trends in machine learning.

Chapter 11.0 Conclusion:

As we draw the curtains on "**Machine Learning Basics for Beginners**," this concluding chapter serves as a recap of key concepts and an encouragement for further exploration. Let's dive into the specifics of each section.

In the journey through the chapters of "Machine Learning Basics for Beginners," we've embarked on a captivating exploration into the heart of one of the most transformative fields in technology. Let's recap the key concepts that we have learnt so far.

1. **Introduction:** We began with our journey into the fascinating realm of Machine Learning Technology, understanding its significance and real-world applications.
2. **Foundations of Machine Learning:** Building a strong foundation, we delved into the core principles and types of machine learning, laying the groundwork for our subsequent chapters.
3. **Data Preprocessing and Feature Engineering:** Unveiling the crucial steps in preparing data for machine learning, we witnessed the power of feature engineering in shaping models.
4. **Building Your First Model:** With newfound knowledge, we took the plunge into constructing our inaugural machine learning model, witnessing the magic unfold in the process.
5. **Supervised Learning Techniques:** We explored the realm of supervised learning, mastering techniques that enable machines to learn from labelled data and make informed predictions.
6. **Unsupervised Learning Techniques:** Venturing into the realm of unsupervised learning, we uncovered the mysteries of clustering and dimensionality reduction, where machines extract patterns from unlabelled data.

7. **Introduction to Deep Learning:** A gateway to the future, we stepped into the world of neural networks, understanding the foundations of deep learning and its transformative potential.

8. **Model Deployment and Production:** Bridging theory with practice, we navigated through the critical phase of deploying models, ensuring their seamless integration into real-world applications.

9. **Ethical and Responsible Machine Learning:** Reflecting on the ethical dimensions of machine learning, we emphasized the importance of fairness, transparency, and responsible AI practices.

10. **Future Trends in Machine Learning:** Peering into the horizon, we glimpsed the exciting trends that promise to shape the future of machine learning, from explainable AI to quantum machine learning.

Encouragement for Further Exploration:

As you close this e-book, consider this not an end but a beginning—a launchpad for your continued exploration into the ever-evolving landscape of machine learning. Armed with foundational knowledge, you stand at the threshold of a realm where curiosity is the compass and innovation know no bounds.

Based on the concepts covered in this e-book, consider how you can apply your newfound knowledge to real-world challenges. Whether you are an aspiring data scientist, a seasoned professional, or an enthusiast, the world of machine learning offers a canvas for innovation and problem-solving. Embrace the curiosity that sparked your journey into this field, and let it propel you toward further discoveries and contributions.

I recommend you to Dive deeper into specific domains, experiment with advanced algorithms, and stay attuned to emerging trends. Join communities, participate in discussions, and learn from both successes and challenges. Remember, the field of machine learning thrives on collaboration, diversity of thought, and a relentless pursuit of understanding. Your curiosity is the engine that propels this journey forward.

Thank you for accompanying me on this exploration of "Machine Learning Basics for Beginners" I hope this e-book has been a valuable resource in your learning journey, and I look forward to the exciting developments you'll contribute to in the dynamic world of machine learning. I encourage you to leave your valuable feedback upon reading this Book, as it motivates and encourages me to deliver more and more innovative and informative topics.

APPENDIX A Glossary of Terms

Artificial Intelligence (AI)

Artificial intelligence is the simulation of human intelligence processes by machines, especially computer systems.

Machine Learning (ML):

A branch of artificial intelligence (AI) that empowers computers to learn patterns and make decisions without explicit programming.

Supervised Learning:

A type of machine learning where the model is trained on labelled data, learning to make predictions or classifications based on input-output pairs.

Unsupervised Learning:

Machine learning paradigm where the model is trained on unlabelled data, discovering patterns, relationships, or structures without predefined outputs.

Deep Learning:

A subset of machine learning utilizing neural networks with multiple layers (deep neural networks) to model complex patterns and representations.

Neural Network:

A computational model inspired by the human brain, consisting of interconnected nodes (neurons) organized in layers to process and learn from data.

Feature Engineering:

The process of selecting, transforming, or creating input features to enhance a machine learning model's performance.

Data Preprocessing:

Cleaning, organizing, and transforming raw data into a suitable format for machine learning, including handling missing values and outliers.

Algorithm:

A set of rules or procedures followed by a computer to solve a particular problem, often used interchangeably with "model" in machine learning.

Model Training:

The phase in machine learning where a model learns from the training data by adjusting its parameters to minimize the difference between predicted and actual outcomes.

Appendix B Recommended Books

I personally gained good amount of knowledge by reading these books and would advise you to read them for acquiring in-depth knowledge on this subject.

Machine Learning for Beginners

✓ Machine Learning For Absolute Beginners: A Plain English Introduction - Oliver Theobald.

✓ The Hundred-Page Machine Learning Book - Andriy Burkov

✓ Machine Learning in Action - Peter Harrington

Advanced Machine Learning Books

✓ Machine Learning for Hackers: Case Studies and Algorithms to Get You Started - Drew Conway

✓ Deep Learning (Adaptive Computation and ML Series) - by Ian Goodfellow, Yoshua Bengio, and Aaron Courville

✓ Pattern Recognition and Machine Learning (Information Science and Statistics) - Christopher M. Bishop

Appendix C Top 15 Jobs that will be in demand in 2024.

In the ever-evolving landscape of Artificial Intelligence (AI), the year 2024 unfolds as a pivotal chapter marked by unprecedented advancements and transformative breakthroughs. AI, once a promising frontier, has now become an integral force shaping industries, societies, and daily life. Here are the Top 15 positions that are going to hit the employment market in 2024.

It is important that we understand the requirement and equip ourself with the updated technology to stand out in the employment market.

1. AI Content Writer
2. AI Prompt Engineer
3. NLP Engineer
4. Computer Vision Engineer
5. Data Analyst
6. AI Software Developer
7. AI Solutions Architect
8. AI Product Manager
9. AI Robotics Engineer
10. AI Ethics Consultant
11. AI Research Scientist:
12. Data Scientist
13. Machine Learning Engineer
14. AI Marketing Specialist
15. Quantum Computing Engineer

Start your journey of learning today and stand out in the technological advancement by 2024.

A Closing Note

Thank you for choosing this book. Our creation gets improved with your opinions. Would be grateful for your valuable feedback!
Suggested Reads :

Visit the Authors Page below to discover our books collection !!!!!
"https://www.amazon.com/author/prabhakarv
For AI enthusiasts who want to stand ahead in AI technology.
Visit our website : https://promthub.blogspot.com/

| Page